PRENTICE HALL

Language Teaching Methodology Series

Classroom Techniques and Resources
General Editor: Christopher N. Candlin

Conversation and Dialogues in Action

Other titles in this series include:

ARGONDIZZO, Carmen
Children in action

FRANK, Christine and RINVOLUCRI, Mario
Grammar in action again

GERNGROSS, Gunter and PUCHTA, Herbert
Pictures in action

GOLEBIOWSKA, Aleksandra
Getting students to talk

GRIFFEE, Dale
Songs in action

McKAY, Sandra
Teaching grammar

NUNAN, David
Language teaching methodology

NUNAN, David
Understanding language classrooms

PECK, Antony
Language teachers at work

ROST, Michael
Listening in action

STEMPLESKI, Susan and TOMALIN, Barry
Video in action

STEVICK, Earl
Success with foreign languages

TAYLOR, Linda
Vocabulary in action

TAYLOR, Linda
Teaching and learning vocabulary

WINGATE, Jim
Getting beginners to talk

YALDEN, Janice
The communicative syllabus

Conversation and Dialogues in Action

ZOLTÁN DÖRNYEI and SARAH THURRELL

Eötvös University, Budapest

ENGLISH LANGUAGE TEACHING

Prentice Hall International
New York London Toronto Sydney Tokyo Singapore

First published 1992 by
Prentice Hall International
Campus 400, Spring Way
Maylands Avenue, Hemel Hempstead
Hertfordshire, HP2 7EZ

Typeset in Times by
MHL Typesetting Ltd, Coventry

Printed and bound in Great Britain by
Redwood Books, Trowbridge, Wiltshire

Library of Congress Cataloging-in-Publication Data

Dörnyei, Zoltán.
    Conversation and Dialogues in Action/Zoltán Dörnyei and Sarah
Thurrell.
        p.   cm. — (English language teaching)
    Includes bibliographical references and indexes.
    ISBN 0-13-175035-6
    1. English language — Study and teaching — Foreign speakers.
2. English language — Spoken English — Study and teaching.
I. Thurrell, Sarah. II. Title. III. Title: Conversation and
Dialogues in Action. IV. Series: English language teaching
(Englewood Cliffs, N.J.)
PE1128.A2D65   1992   92-12368
428′.007 — dc20   CIP

British Library Cataloguing in Publication Data

A catalogue record for this book is available
from the British Library

ISBN 0-13-175035-6

9 8 7 6 5 4
1999 98 97 96

Contents

Preface

Within the Language Teaching Methodology Series we have created a special set of books with the *In Action* title. These books are designed to offer teachers material that can be directly used in class. They offer language teachers material which can be adapted with various inputs for their own classroom work. The activities are accessible and user-friendly, with a clear identification of teacher and learner roles, and, above all, they consist of tried and tested tasks. The authors of the books in the *In Action* collection all have considerable practical experience of teaching and of classroom research. It is this combination of principle and practice, available in an easily digestible form for the teacher, which characterises the design of the books.

Conversation and Dialogues in Action is in many ways the classic book in the *In Action* collection: it rediscovers and revitalises a traditional classroom activity, and structures it for classroom use. Developing conversational skills is very often seen as a filler among other more structured activities in class, partly because we have not seen talking as the structured and rule-governed activity it is. Fortunately, through recent work in discourse analysis and pragmatics, descriptions of everyday conversation now abound, including many that are drawn from non-native speaker interactions. What we have largely lacked, however, until this exciting contribution to the series from Zoltan Dornyei and Sarah Thurrell, is a way in which descriptions can be transformed into classroom tasks in a principled way.

This book breaks down conversation into its own grammar, showing how people open and close conversations, take turns at talking, interrupt and reformulate what others say. We use a range of conversational tactics, largely subconsciously, but these characterise perhaps more than any other skill our competence in our own and in a foreign language. But the book is not just about finding out how conversation works; its chief purpose is to help teachers develop that competence in their learners.

The tasks suggest a great range of ways in which learners can work together on conversational tasks in class. After all, conversation is characteristically cooperative; it is a joint and even a group activity! So it offers tremendous potential for reorganising the social structure of the classroom to foster more learner-centered activity.

As General Editor, I hope that the books in the *In Action* collection will continue the success of the Language Teaching Methodology Series in developing the skills and knowledge of the reflective language teacher in the classroom.

Professor Christopher N Candlin
General Editor

Acknowledgements

We would like to say how grateful we are to Isobel Fletcher de Téllez and David Haines from Prentice Hall International: without their faith in us and their encouragement and support — not to mention their inspiring suggestions and comments — CONVERSATION AND DIALOGUES IN ACTION, which is partly their own brainchild, might never have been written — at least not by us!

We are also greatly indebted to our Series Editor, Professor Christopher Candlin, for putting us on the right track with regard to the theoretical background and presentation format of the book, and also for his valuable comments on earlier drafts which played a crucial role in shaping the present book.

We would also like to express our warm thanks to Marianne Celce-Murcia, who first introduced us to conversation analysis, and to Lynne Young for her helpful advice.

Special thanks are due to Emese Koppány, Nelli Szakács and Ildikó Szigeti, who piloted the manuscript and gave us detailed feedback on the activities. Their invaluable suggestions resulted in many improvements being made.

Finally, we would like to thank our own students for being 'guinea-pigs', knowingly or unknowingly, for the purpose of developing the activities in the book.

Introduction

Even the best language learners often complain that they feel at a loss when meeting native speakers and engaging in real-life **CONVERSATION**.

Nowadays, language teaching coursebooks present a great deal of their new material through **DIALOGUES**.

Modern language teaching theory stresses that learning is fastest through doing. Therefore it is important to let students see the language we teach **IN ACTION**.

CONVERSATION AND DIALOGUES IN ACTION is a collection of communicative activities to teach *conversational skills* in a foregin/second language by exploiting *instructional dialogues*. The ideas in the book can be used to supplement coursebook-based teaching at all levels, or to form the basis of special conversation classes. A unique feature of CONVERSATION AND DIALOGUES IN ACTION is that it translates current linguistic theory into practice: the classroom activities offer lifelike practice in the rules of 'conversational grammar' as defined by research in the last decade, and the inputs provide rich and systematic collections of conversational phrases and structures that students need.

Conversation and conversational skills

Many people believe that informal everyday conversation is random and unstructured. This is, in fact, far from true. Although conversation may take many forms and the speakers and situations vary widely, all conversation follows certain patterns. There are, for example, subtle rules determining who speaks and when and for how long. Thanks to these rules, the participants in a conversation take turns with astonishing precision: there is hardly any overlap or simultaneous talk.

There are also rituals and set formulae for starting or closing a conversation and for changing the subject; there are conventions prescribing how to interrupt and how to hold the floor, and even determining what style is most appropriate in a given situation. These conventions are fairly strong and consistent within a given culture: when someone breaks them, people can tell immediately that something has gone wrong.

The analysis of the rules that govern conversation has been of major interest to linguists over the last two decades. Now we know that conversation is a highly organised activity which requires definite skills on the part of the speakers. Learners may be familiar with the grammar of a language, may know a vast amount of vocabulary, and can still 'fail', that is, let themselves down in real conversation. Speaking skills are not enough: spontaneous, on-line interaction in a social setting, with partners to listen and react to, requires additional competence. CONVERSATION AND DIALOGUES IN ACTION aims to develop this competence.

How to teach conversational skills

Can conversational skills be taught specifically? Or do they come automatically with exposure to the target language? In the last fifteen years, teaching experts have tended to favour the latter hypothesis. It was assumed that conversational skills could be acquired through doing communicative activities such as situational role-plays, problem-solving tasks and information-gap exercises. While these certainly do help students to become better conversationalists, it has been suggested recently that traditional communicative activities could be combined to better effect with a *more direct approach* to the teaching of conversational skills.

   This direct approach would involve fostering the students' awareness of conversation and increasing their sensitivity to the underlying processes. In other words, if learners are conscious of the strategies they could use and the pitfalls they should avoid, and if they have a wide repertoire of set expressions and conversational formulae on hand, they are likely to make much faster progress towards becoming relaxed and polished conversationalists. CONVERSATION AND DIALOGUES IN ACTION has been written to provide material for this more direct method of teaching conversational skills.

Teaching dialogues: Why and how?

If we wish to develop language learners' communicative competence in foreign or second languages, we need to present language material which can be readily used in communication. And even though textbook dialogues are often only simplistic and contrived imitations of real-life conversation, they do provide the learners with basic communicative experiences, for the following reasons:

   They offer a functional, situational presentation of the new material, illustrating its communicative role.
   They allow for timesaving, intensive practice by highlighting and clarifying certain items.
   They *seem* more authentic because they introduce different speakers, different styles of speaking and different conversational topics, and therefore students typically find them more lively and more interesting than narrative texts.
   They lend themselves to further, less structured exploitation.

For these reasons, current language teaching textbooks and other teaching materials are based, to a considerable extent, on dialogues, and therefore a lot of what is happening in the language classroom nowadays is centred around instructional dialogues.

CONVERSATION AND DIALOGUES IN ACTION aims to bring these dialogues to life and bridge the gap between textbook-bound, contrived classroom talk and real conversation. The teaching principle of the book is to provide structured guidelines (as well as actual language input) to depart from the instructional texts which function as raw material, and to take learners towards spontaneous and creative communication.

Teachers who do not have a prescribed lesson-to-lesson syllabus or a compulsory coursebook can also use the book by finding, inventing, or even recording dialogues to provide the starting point, or by getting their students to produce role-play sketches which can be further elaborated on in these activities.

The structure of the book

CONVERSATION AND DIALOGUES IN ACTION is divided into four main sections:

Section I:	Conversational rules and structure
Section II:	Conversational strategies
Section III:	Functions and meanings in conversation
Section IV:	Social and cultural contexts

Each section focuses on a different aspect of conversation and is introduced by a short text which summarises the issues dealt with and the topic areas the activities tackle. The following is a very brief summary of the main themes of the sections:

Section I is centred around **Conversational rules and structures**, that is, how conversation is organised, and what prevents conversations from continually breaking down into a chaos of interruptions and simultaneous talk. Among others, there are activities to teach students how to start and keep up informal conversation (**1 Relax and chat**), how to change the subject smoothly (**2 By the way, that reminds me**), how to break into a conversation politely (**3 Sorry to interrupt**) and how to bring a conversation tactfully to a close (**10 It was nice talking to you**).

Section II focuses on **Conversational strategies**, that is, ways and means of helping speakers to overcome communication breakdowns, to deal with trouble spots, and to enhance fluency. Students can learn, among other things, how to gain time by using fillers and hesitation devices (**11 Buying time: fillers**), how to ask for repetition in order to clarify meaning (**12 Pardon?**), how to paraphrase when they don't remember a word (**17 The thing you open bottles with**), and how to make their narrative style more dynamic (**20 You'll never believe this!**).

Section III concentrates on **Functions and meanings in conversation**, that is, message and purpose. Several of the activities deal with the main language functions of conversation (**22 Questions and answers, 23 Oh yes, I agree**, etc.), offering an array of function-specific expressions and structures. Students are also made aware that different language forms can have the same meaning (**26 Change without changing**), that the literal meaning of certain structures is not the same as the real meaning (**27 What they say and what they mean**), and that one sentence can have several meanings (**28 Paranoia or a hidden meaning in everything**).

Section IV leads into broader issues by focusing on how **Social and cultural contexts** affect conversation. Some of the issues tackled are, for example, how a person's status and personality is reflected in conversation (**30 Who is the new one?**), the main features of politeness (**32 Let's not be so polite!**), and when and how to use formal and informal style (**33 Formal−informal**). Attention is also drawn to the fact that different cultures have different conversational customs; language learners often face communication difficulties because of differing cultural backgrounds; therefore a sensitivity to crosscultural issues is a prerequisite of becoming an efficient conversationalist (**36 Cultural differences and taboos, 37 Visitor from Mars**).

The activities

Although the activities are divided into four sections, they all exist independently of each other (which means, for example, that an activity from the end of the book can easily be done without first going through the ones before it). These activities are presented in a 'recipe' format and are introduced by four headings:

Level	recommended level of language proficiency needed; we have distinguished three levels: elementary, intermediate and advanced.
Purpose	the teaching purpose of the activity, i.e., the conversational issue the activity tackles.
Dialogue type	what kind of dialogue can best be used as the starting point of the activity.
In this activity	a brief description of what students do in the activity.

Then comes the actual activity, which includes Preparation (for the teacher) and In class stages, both of which are broken down into step-by-step instructions.

The majority of the activities contain Sample dialogues to illustrate the task and INPUTS of expressions/phrases to teach to the students (see **E. List of input boxes of conversational phrases** in the Indexes). Note that the structures listed in these inputs are written in an economical format, e.g., *'Could/Can/Would you repeat that (for me), please?'*, which is, in fact, three different expressions in one, and each of them has two possible variations depending on whether the optional *'for me'* is used. We believe that this format may be confusing for students and we therefore suggest that you select *some* phrases from the lists and introduce the structures in their complete form, e.g., *'Would you repeat that please?'*, *'Could you repeat that for me, please?'*, etc.

Each activity is followed by **Follow-up options** (providing further exploitation of the material), one or two **Variations** (offering alternative activities focusing on the same theme), and **Links** (pointing out other related activities in the book which would logically follow on from the one in question).

At the end of each activity is a **Teacher's diary**, which contains questions addressed to you, the teacher, in order to provide a framework to evaluate

how the activity went;
what the student's reactions were and why;
which parts turned out to be too difficult or too easy;
how the student's first language and cultural background influenced the activity, etc.

We would like to encourage you to spend some time reflecting on the classroom activities in this way, perhaps even to take notes, and this could be taken further and turned into a kind of action research. The results could then be used to give added direction to your teaching and to your students' learning.

How to use the book

CONVERSATION AND DIALOGUES IN ACTION can be used in different ways, depending on whether you (the teacher) follow a coursebook or not.

1   Using the book to supplement your coursebook
Since the activities in the book have been designed to be used with instructional dialogues, CONVERSATION AND DIALOGUES IN ACTION makes it possible to include conversation practice in the lessons while closely following the course syllabus and the official coursebook. This is something which, as teachers know, is usually quite difficult to organise. By using the **Indexes** at the back of the book, you can select tasks that best emphasise or compliment the teaching point of the unit/dialogue you are working with. Or you can select an activity which would work well with the topic of the current textbook dialogue.

There are five indexes to help you:

A. The teaching purpose of the activities (in order of appearance in the book)
B. Short summaries of the activities (in alphabetical order)
C. Activities by language proficiency level
D. Subject index
E. List of input boxes of conversational phrases

2 Using the book for conversation classes without a set coursebook

If you are relatively free to write your own syllabus and you do not use a set coursebook, CONVERSATION AND DIALOGUES IN ACTION can be used to structure conversation classes in two ways:

Using the **Indexes** (see above), you can select an activity you want your students to do, then find (e.g., in coursebooks and supplementary materials), write or record a dialogue which can function as the starting point. In order to facilitate this approach, we have described at the beginning of each activity under **Dialogue type** what kind of dialogue best lends itself to that activity.

You can combine the activities in the book with situational role-plays: choose a role-play situation which suits the activity you want to do and get your students to act it out. They have then created the dialogue which becomes the basis of the conversation activity.

NOTE: *If you use printed dialogues, most activities will work better if the students are already familiar with the text, e.g., they have covered the new grammar points or vocabulary.*

Further reading and teaching resources

Background reading

Brown, G. and Yule, G.: *Teaching the Spoken Language*. Cambridge: Cambridge University Press, 1983.

A thorough and clear theoretical introduction to the features of spoken English, written in an accessible style. It also covers the practical implications of the theory described, with separate chapters devoted to the teaching and assessment of oral production and listening comprehension.

Cook, G.: *Discourse*. Oxford: Oxford University Press, 1989.

This concise and easy-to-read book gives an excellent summary of the complete theory of discourse analysis (including conversation analysis), and is geared to the practising teacher. If you only have time to read one book on the theoretical background, then we would say this is it!

David Crystal: *The Cambridge Encyclopedia of Language*. Cambridge: Cambridge University Press, 1987.

This encyclopedia covers all aspects of language and language use, not just conversation. However, it provides such excellent (and short!) summaries of every topic that it is a real treasure-trove for the overburdened language teacher. A special feature is the rich selection of interesting examples to illustrate the theoretical points.

Richards, J. C.: *Conversationally speaking: approaches to the teaching of conversation*. In: Richards, J. C.: *The Language Teaching Matrix*, 1990, pp. 67—86.

Jack C. Richards was one of the pioneers of applying conversation analysis to language teaching and has played an important part in establishing a more systematic approach to communicative teaching. This paper summarises the theory of conversation analysis from a practical perspective. Incredibly instructive in only 19 pages!

Robinson, G. L. N.: *Crosscultural Understanding*. Hemel Hempstead: Prentice Hall, 1988.
'How can a person from one culture understand someone from another?' In order to answer this question, the author examines issues like what culture is; what the effects of cultural experiences are; how negative cultural perceptions can be modified and positive impressions facilitated, etc. We become familiar with psychological, anthropological and ethnographical theories, which are made lifelike by accounts of the author's rich personal experiences, both in crosscultural communication and language teaching.

Scarcella, R. C., Andersen, E. S. and Krashen, S. D. (eds.): *Developing Communicative Competence in a Second Language*. New York: Newbury House, 1990.
This book is a collection of nineteen research articles on various aspects of teaching and acquiring communicative competence, with separate chapters examining sociolinguistic, discourse and strategic competencies. The range of topics is impressive and the final five studies specifically address the teaching of communication in the classroom. Contributors include some of the most wellknown North-American and Dutch applied linguists.

Smith, L. E. (ed.): *Discourse Across Cultures; Strategies in World Englishes*. Hemel Hempstead: Prentice Hall, 1987.
This edited volume consists of thirteen articles centred around crosscultural communication and English as an international language. The wide selection of topics covered ranges from Japanese—American cultural differences to cultural barriers in the language classroom. Contributors include world experts such as Christopher Candlin, Braj and Yamuna Kachru, Elaine Tarone, Henry Widdowson and George Yule.

Tarone, E. and Yule, G.: *Focus on the Language Learner*. Oxford: Oxford University Press, 1989.
This well structured and informative book gives a clear overview of what language knowledge involves (including concise and highly readable summaries of the components of communicative competence!), what the language learner's needs are, and finally how to carry out research on the learner.

Teaching resources

Blundell, J., Higgens, J. and Middlemiss, N.: *Function in English*. Oxford: Oxford University Press, 1982.
An extremely rich resource book containing over 3000 different English structures divided into 140 functional, social and communicative categories. What is more, the structures are also classified according to how formal they are, and there are practice exercises.

Golębiowska, A.: *Getting Students to Talk*. Hemel Hempstead: Prentice Hall, 1990.
This books kills as many as three birds with one stone: Firstly, it sets out systematic guidelines for classroom management in a communicative class, secondly it contains a nice collection of role-plays, simulations and discussion activities, and thirdly (very rare in such recipe books) it provides detailed language input for each activity, consisting of useful structures and conversational formulae. Just what a practising teacher needs!

Jones, L.: *Functions of English*. Cambridge: Cambridge University Press, 1981.
A classic which has come out in two editions and many printings. A functional course (containing chapters on conversation techniques, narrative techniques and dialogue handling) with a lot of cassette recordings and communicative tasks.

Keller, E. and Taba-Warner, S.: *Gambits; Conversational Tools*; Vol. I: *Openers*, Vol. II: *Links*, Vol. III: *Responders, Closers & Inventory*. Ottawa: Public Commission of Canada, 1976, 1979.

(Now also published by Hove: Language Teaching Publications, under the title of *Conversation Gambits*.)

These three slim volumes contain a wealth of useful conversational phrases and routines, organised along the main aspects of conversational functions. The phrases are accompanied by highly imaginative and well structured communicative ideas, suggesting how students can put them into practice. *Gambits* is an invaluable asset to the conversational class.

Nolasco, R. and Arthur, L.: *Conversation*. Oxford: Oxford University Press, 1987.

A very rich collection of communicative activities, explicitly based on the theory of conversational analysis. Clear presentation, lots of practical advice, a great deal of materials to photocopy (legally!) for the students — all in all, this book is a must for the communicative teacher.

SECTION I

CONVERSATIONAL RULES AND STRUCTURE

Introduction

As we pointed out in the general Introduction, conversation is in fact a highly organised activity, exhibiting distinct patterns and regularities. The following is a brief overview of some key issues of conversation analysis which feature in Section I and an indication of the activities which focus on them.

Openings

Conversations do not simply begin at random; there are various ways of starting a conversation and most of these are fairly ritualised as, for example, in different sequences of greetings and introductions. There are also some accepted ways of how to initiate a chat and various strategies (which students often don't know) of how to turn a brief factual exchange (e.g., buying something in a shop) into an informal conversation (**1 Relax and chat**).

Turn-taking

How do people know when to speak in conversations so that they do not talk at the same time as the other(s)? There are, in fact, some subtle rules and signals to determine who talks, when, and for how long; if there were not, conversation would constantly break down. Researchers have labelled these rules *turn-taking mechanisms* since they organise how participants in conversation take turns to speak. Unfortunately, the language classroom does not offer too many opportunities for students to develop their awareness of turn-taking rules and to practise turn-taking skills. However, for many students (especially for those coming from cultures whose turn-taking conventions are very different from in the target language) turn-taking ability does not come automatically and therefore needs to be developed consciously (**7 Turn-taking in conversation**).

Interrupting

One special case in turn-taking is interrupting, which is a definite conversational *don't* in many cultures. In English, a certain amount of interruption is tolerated (especially when the purpose is to sort out some problem of understanding), but too much appears rude. Interruptions are almost always introduced by set phrases, which provide polite and natural ways of performing this rather delicate task. Students should be familiar with these (**3 Sorry to interrupt**).

Adjacency pairs

There are some utterances, e.g., questions, invitations, requests, apologies, compliments, etc., which require an immediate response or reaction from the communication partner. These utterances and their responses (together) are known by linguists as *adjacency pairs*. A special feature of adjacency pairs is that after the first speaker's utterance, two different reactions are usually possible from the other speaker:

1   an expected, polite reaction, e.g., accept an invitation, comply with a request,
2   an unexpected or less common reaction, e.g., turn down an invitation, refuse to comply with a request.

The two types of reactions have been called *preferred* and *dispreferred answers* respectively. Just like native speakers, language learners typically find dispreferred answers much more difficult to produce, partly because they are more difficult languagewise: in many cultures when you give a dispreferred answer, you must be tactful, must be indirect in order not to sound rude, you need to apologise and offer justifications, and for language learners these require practice (**9 I'm afraid I can't**).

Conversational routines
A typical feature of natural conversation is the wide use of fixed expressions or *conversational routines*. These are what make conversation rich. Polished conversationalists are in command of hundreds, if not thousands, of such phrases and use them, for example, to break smoothly into a conversation, to hold the listeners interest, to change the subject, to react to what others say, and to step elegantly out of the conversation when they wish. Such routines and structures can be taught explicitly, and we have therefore made a special point of including comprehensive lists of them throughout the book (see index **E. List of input boxes of conversational phrases** at the back of the book).

Topic shift
A typical example of a situation when conversational routines come in very handy is when you want to change the subject, either because you do not want to talk about a certain thing any longer or because you want to introduce a new topic (**2 By the way, that reminds me**). In fact, skimming over a considerable number of topics in a short span of time is a characteristic feature of informal conversation.

Closings
Unless we want to be deliberately rude, we cannot end a conversation by simply saying, 'Well, that's all I want to say, bye', or just hang up the phone abruptly without any notice. Instead, people typically apply a sequence of *pre-closing* and *closing formulae* to prepare the ground for ending a conversation. Language learners can easily misunderstand the closing signals other speakers make and they themselves often lack a sufficient repertoire of such closing routines to be able to conclude and leave without sounding abrupt. That is why it is important to teach closing strategies explicitly (**10 It was nice talking to you**).

This section also contains activities which focus on the internal organisation and coherence of conversation (**5 Dialogue halves, 6 Jumbled dialogue**) and on a combination of several of the microskills discussed above (**4 I haven't got all day!, 8 I couldn't get a word in edgeways!**).

1 Relax and chat

Level   Intermediate and advanced

Purpose   Develop ability to start and keep up informal conversation

Dialogue type   Dialogue containing short, factual exchanges between two people, e.g., between a salesperson and a customer

In this activity

Students turn a short, factual exchange into a conversation by carrying it on, broadening the topic and developing a social relationship between the speakers.

Preparation

1. Find a short factual exchange, and prepare a sample version of it in which the speakers do not stop once the purpose of the dialogue has been fulfilled but rather carry on chatting. You may use the sample dialogue.

Sample dialogue

Original

Customer: Two pounds of tomatoes, please.
Greengrocer: Here you are, sir. That'll be 90p please.
Customer: Thank you.
Greengrocer: 10p change. Thank you sir. Goodbye.
Customer: Goodbye.

Extended, chatty version

Customer: Two pounds of tomatoes, please.
Greengrocer: Here you are, sir. That'll be 90p and cheap at the price!
Customer: Yes, they look like good ones. It would be cheaper still if I grew my own. My garden's just about big enough.
Greengrocer: Well you could, sir, but it's a lot of trouble, you know. You need special soil, fertilisers, a greenhouse.
Customer: Well yes, and I suppose that would cost money.
Greengrocer: It certainly would, sir. And why bother when you can get two pounds of tomatoes from me for only 90p, eh?

INPUT 1　Typical conversation starters

| Excuse me,
Forgive me for asking,
I hope you don't mind me asking,
(I'm) sorry (to trouble you), | but | is anyone sitting here?
do you know if the Bath train's
　left?
aren't you Marjorie Pickering's
　son?
haven't we met somewhere
　before?
could I borrow your . . . ? |

Other questions

Have you got the time please? / How old is the little dog? / Not many people today, are there? / Do you come here often? / Have you heard (the news) about . . . ? / etc.

Weather

At last some nice weather . . . / Lovely day, isn't it? / etc.

Making a comment on something present

Those are lovely apples . . . / etc.

Opening complaints

The traffic in this city is simply incredible . . . / The service on this line is getting worse and worse . . . / Can you believe it? The price of . . . has gone up again! / etc.

Asking for a small favour

Could you please tell me what this says, I'm afraid my eyesight isn't too good. / Could you please watch my suitcase for a moment? / etc.

Party lines

Great party, isn't it? / Hello! Are you a friend of David's? / etc.

2. Collect a number of typical phrases or sentences which people might use to strike up a conversation with a stranger. Some that we thought of are listed in INPUT 1.

In class

1. Present the original factual dialogue and the extended, chatty version you have prepared. Discuss with the students which of the two would be more common when a language learner is one of the speakers and why.

2. Ask students to brainstorm phrases people could use to start a conversation and make a list of these on the board (including the ones you have collected).

3. Point out that the other speaker can encourage the person who starts the chat (a) by not simply answering 'yes' or 'no' but adding a comment, or (b) asking further questions. In this way, the conversation can go on.

4. Students get into pairs and each pair prepares an extended version of the original short dialogue by making the speakers get involved in a chat rather than just complete their business quickly.

5. The groups act out the versions and so the class can see several ways of how one particular situation can be made to include some real, open-ended conversation.

Follow-up options

1. For homework, ask the students to look for 'chat-starting' sentences in other dialogues, books or films. Then, in pairs, they choose a situation and present it to the class, describing the way the first speaker initiated the chat and how the other went along with it.

2. Together as a class, collect 'chat-starting' sentences and phrases under three headings: ones that can be used between (a) strangers in the street or on the train, bus, etc., (b) neighbours or colleagues, (c) working people e.g., shopkeepers, postpeople, repairmen, and their customers.

3. Students do the activity in reverse: find or record a dialogue which is full of informal chat and ask them to reduce it to a short, factual exchange.

Variation 1   Keep the conversation going

Sitting in a circle, students practise strategies to keep the conversation going by following one or more of the following four 'conversational patterns':

1. Student 1 (S1) asks a question; S2 answers it, elaborates on the answer, then asks a related question; S3 answers it, etc.
2. S1 expresses an opinion; S2 agrees with it and expresses a related opinion; S3 agrees, etc.

3. S1 relates some interesting facts or news; S2 reacts to it and then adds his/her own facts, news, etc.
4. S1 says a sentence which can be anything; S2 reacts to it and asks a question concerning this sentence; S3 answers and elaborates on the subject; S4 reacts and asks a further question about the same topic, etc.

Variation 2   Let's not chat

Sometimes when you are absolutely *not* in the mood to have a chat you find yourself with someone who is very eager to share their views on anything with you. What can you do? In such situations people typically try to be as short and unresponsive as possible without being offensive. Ask students in pairs to perform a situation in which the 'intruder' cannot and will not be put off by the lack of reactions or the odd blunt response, and so the dialogue becomes a series of conversation starters and short but polite refusals.

Link

Consider trying **By the way, that reminds me (2)** from this section, and **Oh yes, I agree (23)** and **Reactions (25)** from the Functions and meanings in conversation section as a follow-up to this activity.

Teacher's diary

Did the 'chat-starting' strategies increase the students' fluency? Which strategies were efficient and which did not work very well for your students?

2 By the way, that reminds me

Level   Intermediate and advanced

Purpose   Develop ability to change the subject naturally

Dialogue type   Any dialogue

In this activity

Students extend the dialogue by introducing new topics.

Preparation

1. Think of a concise description of the subject of the dialogue you are going to have with your class, e.g., (discussing) the arrangements of a party.

2. (For the Follow-up options) Think up some other conversational topics (preferably unusual ones!) and write them on cue cards.

In class

1. Ask the class to describe in one sentence what the dialogue is about. Then get them to brainstorm some other, perhaps more unusual, topics which they would like to see dealt with in a coursebook. Make a list on the board/OHP.

2. Point out that during the course of real-life conversation, people often keep moving on to different topics and usually use set phrases to do this, e.g. *'by the way'*. Elicit more such phrases from them and suggest some yourself (see INPUT 2). Draw up a list on the board.

3. Get the students into small groups or pairs (depending on the number of characters in the dialogue). To make the activity more challenging, each group is to pick out one topic from the board for another group, e.g. with three groups: Group A for Group B, Group B for Group C, and Group C for Group A, and the groups prepare a new version of the dialogue by including the topic they have been given.

INPUT 2   Changing the subject in a conversation

(Oh) by the way . . .
That reminds me (of) . . .
Speaking about/of . . . / Talking of . . .
Before I forget . . . / Oh, I nearly forgot! . . .
Oh, while I remember . . .
I just thought of something . . .
Oh, there's something else I wanted/meant to say . . . / ask you . . .
Oh, I knew there was something I meant/wanted to tell you . . .
Oh I know what I wanted/meant to say . . . / tell/ask you . . .
This has got nothing to do with what we are talking about, but . . .
I know this is changing the subject but . . .
Changing the subject (for a minute) . . .
Funny/Strange you should mention/say that . . .
That's funny, because something similar . . .
Incidentally, . . .

4. The groups extend the dialogue by making the characters introduce and start talking about the topic they have been given, using one or more of the phrases listed on the board.

5. Students perform their extended versions of the dialogue. The audience notes down which phrases they chose to change the subject and what subjects were covered (they could do this by writing down keywords).

Follow-up options

1. Give each group several cue cards with different topics on them so the dialogue becomes a series of topic shifts.

2. This time, each participant is given (or draws) a cue card just before the performance. They must improvise so that they include the topic on the card in the performance.

3. You may want to have students practise how to return to the original topic after being side-tracked (see INPUT 3).

Variation 1   Stopping Uncle Freddy

In groups, students adjust the dialogue so that one speaker is Uncle Freddy, who is extremely talkative and gets side-tracked all the time, constantly changing the subject, whereas the other speaker(s) would like to get on with the original conversation. How long can Uncle Freddy prevent the dialogue from ending?

Variation 2   Change-the-subject chain

Prepare cue cards with different topics on them and let everybody pick one at random. Students sit in a circle. The teacher starts talking about any topic, inviting one of the students to join in. At some point the student, using phrases from INPUT 2, should change the subject to talk about one of his/her topics, inviting the next student to join in . . . Go on until all the students have had a turn. This can also be done in smaller groups, which gives each student more opportunity to speak and may make the task less stressful.

Link

Consider trying **Relax and chat (1)** and **I haven't got all day! (4)** from this section, and **Going off the point (19)** from the Conversational strategies section as a follow-up to this activity.

Teacher's diary

Are the strategies for changing the subject different in the students' native language(s) than in English? Is it common and socially acceptable to change the subject like that? Which phrases did students find most useful?

3 Sorry to interrupt

Level   Elementary and above

Purpose   Develop turn-taking skills in conversation; practise smooth
                     interruptions

Dialogue type   Dialogue containing longer turns

In this activity

Students use interrupting strategies to break into a conversation several times.

Preparation

1. Find or make a recorded monologue (any topic).

2. Prepare a list of 4–5 phrases your students can use when they want to interrupt
    a conversation and when they want to return to the original topic (see INPUT 3).

INPUT 3   Interrupting a conversation and then returning to the topic

To interrupt

(I'm) sorry to interrupt . . .
Sorry to break in, but . . .
Sorry, can/may I interrupt you for
  a second . . .
Excuse me . . . / Pardon me . . .
Excuse/Pardon me for interrupting,
  but . . .
If I may interrupt for a second . . .
Sorry, but did I hear you say
  . . . ?
I couldn't help overhearing . . .

To return

As I was saying . . .
(Now) what was I saying / what
  were we talking about . . . ?
Where was I . . . ?
Going back to . . .
To return to / Going back to what
  I was saying before . . .
To get back to what we were
  talking about . . .
Let's get back to . . .
(Yes, well) anyway . . .
In any case . . .

---

3. Go through the dialogue you will be using with your students and think of some possible characters who could be added to play the role of nuisance and constantly interrupt the others; some possibilities are: a clever-clever teenager, a know-all relative, the boss or a nosy colleague, a drunk person sitting nearby, etc.

In class

1. Without any introduction, start playing your recording and try to interrupt the speaker using several of the interrupting phrases. Then pause and ask the students what you were trying to do and which phrases they can remember. Continue with the recording, this time with the students noting down your words.

2. Elicit any other phrases students know for interrupting a conversation and put these up on the board/OHP, along with the ones you have introduced. Do the same with phrases to return to the topic after being interrupted.

3. Divide the students into small groups so that there are enough people in each group for the roles in the dialogue plus one extra who will be the interrupter. Tell them that their task will be to perform the dialogue with one of them constantly interrupting it, using the phrases they have collected.

4. The groups decide who will play the role of the interrupter, then work out this new character's identity and relationship with the other participants. To give them ideas, tell them about the characters you thought of.

5. The interrupter must use at least four different ways of interrupting; all the group members help to invent these new lines. The other character(s) will have to return to the topic, using a different phrase each time.

6. Students perform the new versions of the dialogue with the interruptions.

Follow-up options

1. Select the interrupters in advance (one for each group). This time they may not consult with the other students who are preparing to act out the original dialogue and therefore some real improvisation will be needed. You may give tips to the interrupters on cue-cards but encourage them to invent some ideas of their own.

2. Ask the students to emphasise body language. Very often someone who wants to interrupt a conversation will first just hang around the people speaking and make obvious body signs, e.g., leaning slightly forward, raising a hand, looking intently at one of the speakers, clearing his/her throat, etc., trying to catch one of the speakers' eye, until the attention is drawn to him/her. Students should collect typical interrupting gestures drawing on their own experience, then perform the dialogues with interruptions. If these gestures seem exaggerated and a bit burlesque, so much the better!

Variation 1   Adding a point

Breaking into a conversation is one type of interruption; another is trying to interrupt someone you are already in conversation with when you want to add a point. Discuss with the students the somewhat different strategies and phrases you can use in such cases (see INPUT 4), then ask them to perform the original dialogue, with the speakers interrupting each other several times to make short additional comments.

INPUT 4   Interrupting phrases to add a point

Hang on ... / Hold on ... / Wait a minute ...
Excuse me ... / Sorry, but ...
Sorry, can I stop you for a second ...
Sorry/Excuse me for interrupting, but ...
Can I just say/add that ...
If I can just add something/make a point here ...
Yes/You're right/I agree, but ...
But surely ...

Variation 2   The interrupting game

Students get into two groups and both are given a short text. Someone from Group A starts reading out the text; Group B's job is to stop them getting to the end for as long as possible by constantly interrupting. After each interruption, Group A must react and return to the text. Afterwards, Group B has a go at reading. The winning team is the one who can delay the end of the other team's text for longer.

Link

Consider trying **By the way, that reminds me (2)**, **I haven't got all day! (4)** and **Turn-taking in conversation (7)** from this section, and **You'll never believe this! (20)** from the Conversational strategies section as a follow-up to this activity.

Teacher's diary

In the students' own culture:

(a)   How acceptable are interruptions, and are there situations in which you must not interrupt?
(b)   Are the body signs used to express the wish to interrupt different?

4 I haven't got all day!

Level   Intermediate and advanced

Purpose   Provide combined practice in skills for initiating a conversation, changing the subject and interrupting (each covered in detail in the units before)

Dialogue type   Any dialogue in which a customer is served or attended to

In this activity

Students modify the original dialogue so that the customer/client gets into a lively conversation with the person attending to him/her, while an impatient second customer tries to interrupt them.

Preparation

1. Before this activity you may want to go through the three previous units with your students, as these provide more thorough practice in the skills to be used here.

2. You may also want to write on the board/OHP some sample sentences that can be used to start a conversation, to change the subject and to interrupt a conversation (see INPUTS 1−3).

In class

1. Ask students whether they have ever been in a situation where they were waiting to be served while the salesperson/attendant was engaged in a lengthy conversation with another customer. Tell them that they are now going to reproduce a scene like this (see **Sample dialogue**).

2. Present the sample sentences you have prepared and quickly revise how one can go about striking up a conversation with somebody, carrying it on by introducing new topics, and how another person can try to interrupt this conversation.

3. Get your students into groups of three. In each group, two students will take the role of the customer and the salesperson in the original dialogue, while the third student will be the new character who is another customer waiting for his/her turn.

4. Students prepare an extended version of the original dialogue along the lines

16

Sample dialogue

1st customer: Could I have three metres of that purple stripy material, please?

Shopkeeper: It is lovely, isn't it? Is it for skirt?

1st customer: No, actually it's for trousers for my daughter ...

Shopkeeper: Really? That's funny, because I nearly made my own daughter some trousers out of that material!

1st customer: That's interesting! How old's your daughter, if you don't mind me asking ...

2nd customer: (Quietly) Er, excuse me, I'm sorry to break in, but ...

Shopkeeper: Jenny? Oh, she'll be sixteen soon. Don't they grow up fast?

1st customer: Yes *don't* they! Talking about growing up, do you know what my son did the other day?

2nd customer: (Louder) Sorry to interrupt, but I'm in a hurry!

Shopkeeper: (To the 2nd customer) Of course, madam, just a minute. (To the 1st customer) That'll be £6.50. What did your son do ... ?

mentioned above. Tell them that the waiting customer should try and interrupt the other two politely first, and then in a more direct and forceful manner.

5. Students perform the new versions of the dialogue.

Follow-up options

1. Ask the students who are watching the performances to take notes and jot down under three headings all the sentences which they thought served the purpose of (a) initiating a chat, (b) changing the subject, and (c) interrupting.

2. Since the situation presented in this unit combines the practice of several important conversational skills, it may be worth further exploiting it by making a real performance of it, with costumes, a furnished scene and props. These can be prepared by the students at home for the next class.

Variation 1   The office game

Ask the students to act out the following situation: Reg has something very important to arrange in an office. He goes there and starts explaining the matter to the person at the desk when her colleague comes in, interrupts the business and the two of them get lost in a lively chat. Reg knows that bureaucrats can be difficult so he tries to interrupt their conversation extremely politely. Finally he succeeds and the secretary is about to return to his problem (for sample sentences to return to the topic, see INPUT 3), when the other official interrupts again . . . etc. Tension gradually builds up and it is for the students to decide how they conclude the dialogue.

Link

Consider trying **Going off the point (19)** from the Conversational strategies section, and **Questions and answers (22)** from the Functions and meanings in conversation section as a follow-up to this activity.

Teacher's diary

Was the situation challenging and involving enough? Did students succeed in using the skills and phrases learnt earlier? What difficulties did they have? Are these skills covered in enough detail in the coursebook(s) you use?

---

5 Dialogue halves

Level   Elementary and above

Purpose   Explore how conversation is structured and sequenced

Dialogue type Any short dialogue with two speakers

In this activity

Half of the students are given a dialogue without Speaker A's part, the other half
without Speaker B's part; they first provide the missing parts, then match these new
dialogue halves.

Preparation

Prepare two skeleton versions of the dialogue: one in which the first speaker's parts
are missing (as in **Skeleton 1** below) and a second in which the other speaker's parts
are left out (as in **Skeleton 2** below).

Sample dialogue skeletons

Skeleton 1

A: . . . .
B: Half past seven.
A: . . . .
B: I'm afraid so.

Skeleton 2

A: What's the time?
B: . . . .
A: Is is that late already?
B: . . . .

In class

1. Students get into pairs. Hand out the dialogue skeletons you have prepared; some
    pairs should be given only Skeleton 1, the others only Skeleton 2.

2. Ask the pairs to write in the missing parts in their dialogue skeletons.

3. Get students into new pairs by joining a student who had Skeleton 1 with another

who had Skeleton 2. Ask them to put together their new dialogue halves, i.e., the parts they have written, and see if the new hybrid dialogue makes any sense. If not, they should make changes that will join the parts together smoothly.

4. Each pair reads out the original hybrid dialogue, then their changed version.

5. After each performance discuss why changes were necessary (if they were).

Follow-up options

1. Ask students to prepare a new version of the missing parts in the skeletons they were originally given. However, this time they can deliberately try to make the text as different from the original version as possible, but so that the dialogue as a whole still makes sense (as in the Skeletons below). Students could then match these halves. The effect will undoubtedly be quite surrealistic and often very funny.

Sample dialogue skeletons

Skeleton 1	Skeleton 2	New hybrid
A: *When is your mother coming?*	A: What's the time?	A: When is your mother coming?
B: Half past seven.	B: *It'll be dark soon.*	B: It'll be dark soon.
A: *Is she bringing your aunt too?*	A: Is it that late already?	A: Is she bringing your aunt too?
B: I'm afraid so.	B: *Why don't you relax?*	B: Why don't you relax?

---

2. Again, prepare half a dialogue, i.e., one speaker's part is left out, but this time scramble the other speaker's bits. Make a copy of this scrambled dialogue half for everyone. In pairs or small groups, students write in the missing part in such a way that the dialogue makes sense.

Variation 1   Multiple-choice dialogue

Take a dialogue and prepare two dialogue halves as described above; however, for each turn in both halves prepare also one or two alternative lines which are similar to the original text but do not quite fit in the dialogue. In this way you have produced two multiple-choice dialogue halves with two or three versions for each turn, out of which only one is correct (see the **Sample dialogue halves**).

In pairs, students get copies of the dialogue halves (one half each) and their task is to read out the dialogue, choosing each time the line which can logically follow what the other speaker has said (the starting line must be given of course!).

Once the students have got the hang of this activity, hand out different dialogues to each pair and ask them this time to prepare the multiple-choice dialogue halves themselves, for the other pairs to perform.

Sample multiple-choice dialogue halves

Original	**Dialogue half A**	**Dialogue half B**
A: What's the time?	A: Is it late? What's the time? Is it seven yet?	A: . . . .
B: Half past seven.	B:	B: It's too late. Half past seven/At half past seven

---

Link

Consider trying activities **Jumbled dialogue (6)** and Variation 1 in **I couldn't get a word in edgeways (8)** from this section, and **Change without changing (26)** from the Functions and meanings in conversation section as a follow-up to this activity.

Teacher's diary

How did the students do in this activity? Do you think this activity helped develop sensitivity to the structuring of dialogues in general?

6   Jumbled dialogue

Level   Elementary and above

Purpose   Develop awareness of the natural and logical organisation
                   within conversation

Dialogue type Any longer dialogue

In this activity

Students rearrange the jumbled parts of a dialogue.

Preparation

Make copies of the dialogue the students will be working with — one for every three
students — and cut them up in such a way that every turn is on a separate slip. Put
the sets of slips together in envelopes.

In class

1. Students get into groups of three. Give each group an envelope.

2. Ask students to shuffle the slips and divide them among themselves. Tell them
   that they *must not* show their slips to the other two.

3. The students' task is to put the slips in the right order by

   first deciding the possible order of their slips,
   each reading out their slip in turn,
   discussing the sequence and agreeing on the order of the slips (without actually
       showing them to each other),
   writing a sequence number on each slip.

4. When all the slips have been numbered, students put together the slips on the
   table in the right order, and read them out to check whether their version and
   the other groups' versions are correct.

Follow-up options

1. A more challenging task is to mix the chunks of two unrelated dialogues in each

envelope so that, as well as deciding the order of the slips, students also have to separate the two dialogues.

2.   Hand out five blank slips to each group and ask them to invent extra lines in the dialogue, i.e., five additional parts to be inserted at different places in the dialogue. Then they should put these back into the envelope together with the original slips, and the groups change envelopes. The task is to reconstruct the dialogue with the extra lines.

Variation 1   Human dialogue chain

Split up the dialogue so that there is a section (or speaker's turn) for every student in the class; write these on separate cards and hand them out to the students. Give them thirty seconds to memorise the section they have got. They then put the slips away, get up and wander around repeating their sequence over and over, and listening carefully to the others. Their task is to find people whose bit could logically come immediately before or after their own. Whenever they hear a possibility, they should jot down that person's name.

Next, the students are asked to form a 'human dialogue chain', i.e., stand in a line according to the order they think the utterances should come in. This might involve some lively negotiation. When they are satisfied with the chain, each student in turn says their line so that they hear the complete dialogue for the first time.

Again, using two unrelated dialogues to form two 'human dialogue chains' gives the exercise an interesting twist.

Link

Consider trying **Dialogue halves (5)** and **Turn-taking in conversation (7)** from this section as a follow-up to this activity.

Teacher's diary

Did your students find this activity easy or difficult? Why? Do you think it is worth repeating it with other dialogues?

---

7 Turn-taking in conversation

Level   Intermediate and advanced

Purpose   Identify the signals people give to coordinate turn-taking in
                     conversation

Dialogue type   A longer, non-factual dialogue, e.g., not a shop scene or
                     waiter—customer talk, which is also available on cassette

In this activity

Students learn about the different signals people use to indicate their turn in a
conversation, then fill in a 'Turn-taking observation sheet' while listening to recorded
dialogues.

Preparation

1. Select a textbook dialogue which contains informal chat/small talk or everyday
    conversation between friends, family, acquaintances, colleagues, etc. Make sure
    that you have the recorded version of it too (a video recording is even better).

2. You will need cassette or video recordings of one or two authentic conversations
    as well if you want to contrast authentic conversation with instructional dialogues.

3. Make a copy of the Turn-taking observation sheet (see INPUT 5) for each student.

In class

1. Discuss with the class why it is that people in conversation hardly ever talk at
    the same time — they take it in turns. How do they know whose turn it is to speak?
    Listen to the beginning of the recording of the dialogue, stopping after each change
    of turn, and discuss what turn-taking signals the speakers gave/received.

2. Get students to think about other possible signals. Hand out the Turn-taking
    observation sheets and go through the items to see if there is anything they have
    not mentioned or anything they can add.

3. The students' next task is to listen to the dialogue again (perhaps twice) and fill
    in the Observation sheet by putting a mark in the proper slot every time a particular

INPUT 5   Turn-taking observation sheet

	Textbook dialogue	Authentic conv.
A speaker gives up his/her turn by		
asking a question from the next speaker		
saying somthing to which a reaction is expected, e.g., a compliment, an offer, a request, etc.		
saying that he/she is finishing, e.g., 'Well, anyway … ', 'So … ', or 'Last but not least … ', etc.		
lowering the pitch or the volume of his/her voice		
slowing down his/her speech		
lengthening the last syllable		
indicating that he/she has finished by laughing		
* indicating that he/she has finished with a facial expression		
* looking at someone		
Other:		
There is an overlap between the turns		
simultaneous talk		
The speaker who takes up the turn		
starts speaking in a natural gap/pause		
signals the wish to speak by using interjections, e.g., 'Mm-hm', 'Yeah', 'Yes, but … ', or 'But listen … ', etc.		
signals the wish to speak with an audible intake of breath		
signals the wish to speak by clearing his/her throat		
interrupts the previous speaker		
completes or adds something to what the previous speaker said, without a pause		
* indicates the wish to speak by making certain movements, e.g., leaning forward, gestures, etc.		
* indicates the wish to speak with a facial expression		
Other:		
* Include these points only if you have a video recording of the conversation		

turn-taking signal occurs. Point out that one change of turn may involve more than one signal.

> NOTE: *Encouraging or 'keep going' noises from the listener, e.g., 'mmm', 'yeah', 'uh-huh', 'right', etc. are not real turns and should not count as simultaneous talk.*

4. After listening to the recordings, discuss the results and sort out the ambiguous points, e.g., whether something is an interruption or just moving briskly into a gap, etc.

5. Play the authentic recording(s). Students continue filling in their Observation sheets (the second column).

6. Compare and contrast the results obtained from the instructional and the authentic conversation.

> NOTE: *One of the main features of instructional dialogues is that the turns are very distinct, i.e., one speaker usually waits till the other has completely finished, which is not always the case in real life.*

Follow-up options

1. Students can repeat the observation process using different authentic recordings in order to be able to work out some general rules about turn-taking. This task can, in fact, be developed into some sort of project work, e.g., looking at different situations like salesperson—customer talk, panel discussion, arguments, etc.

2. Discuss with the students how the turn-taking signals vary when a discussion gets more and more heated. Are there any individual turn-taking characteristics, e.g., one person often interrupts others?

Variation 1   The turn-taking game

Students work in pairs/small groups depending on the number of characters in the dialogue. First they go through the different ways of turn-taking as listed in the Turn-taking observation sheet (see INPUT 5). Then each pair or group prepares a new version of the dialogue in which they include all the listed turn-taking signals but one. Students in the audience must find the missing one, which they can only do if they fill in an Observation sheet during the performances.

Link

Consider trying **Sorry to interrupt (3)** and **I couldn't get a word in edgeways (8)** from this section, and **Reactions (25)** from the Functions and meanings in conversation section as a follow-up to this activity.

Teacher's diary

How difficult did students find identifying the turn-taking signals? Did the comparison of textbook dialogues and authentic conversation produce any interesting and/or useful results? Are these signals different in the students' own language and culture?

8 I couldn't get a word in edgeways

Level Intermediate and advanced

Purpose Focus on the differences between dialogues and monologues

Dialogue type Any dialogue with two speakers

In this activity

Students turn the dialogue into a monologue by making one speaker do all the talking, not giving the other a chance to speak.

Preparation

1. Take a short dialogue (two or three exchanges) and rewrite it as a monologue by making the first speaker very talkative (see **Sample dialogue**, Version 1).

Sample dialogue

Original

A: Great party, isn't it. I like barbecues, don't you?
B: Yes. It's so nice to be outside on summer evenings.
A: I'm going to get another hot dog. Shall I bring you one, too?
B: Oh, no thanks. I've had three already.

Version 1 (monologue)

A: Great party, isn't it. I like barbecues, don't you? Yes, I'm sure you do; I mean, who *wouldn't* enjoy being outside on a beautiful summer evening like this, eh?
B: Yes . . .
A: Look, I'm going to get another hot dog. I don't suppose you'd like one, though, would you, since you've already had three! It's easy to eat too much at parties like this, isn't it . . .

---

2. Write these two versions of the dialogue on the board/OHP.

In class

1. Present the material you have prepared. Ask students whether they have met people who behave like the first speaker, and discuss such situations briefly. An alternative presentation would be to go into class and start talking continuously, asking questions and not waiting for the answers, etc.

2. In pairs, students turn the dialogue into a monologue in which the first speaker talks for both of them and the second can't get a word in edgeways (see **Sample dialogue**, Version 1).

3. The pairs perform their versions. Afterwards, discuss why the first speaker's behaviour is unacceptable in conversation.

Follow-up option

Students rewrite the dialogue so that the *other* speaker gets a turn to dominate the conversation.

Variation 1   One-sided telephone conversation

In pairs, students turn the dialogue into a telephone conversation, perhaps by reporting it as if at a later time (see **Sample dialogue**, Version 2). They then rewrite the conversation as if for a television play, where you can only hear one speaker and yet can guess exactly what the other is saying (see **Sample dialogue**, Version 3). As each pair performs their one-sided conversation, the others write down what they think the other speakers said.

Sample dialogue

Version 2 (telephone conversation)
A: Did you enjoy the barbecue last night?
B: Yes, it was lovely. And the weather was so mild! I didn't even need my jumper.
A: No, neither did I. And I ate so much!
B: Don't talk to me about that! I had three hot dogs and two slices of cheesecake.
A: Oh, never mind. You have to enjoy yourself sometimes, don't you.

Version 3 (one-sided telephone conversation)
A: Did you enjoy the barbecue last night? ... Incredibly warm, wasn't it? I didn't wear mine either. And I ate so much! ... *How* many hot dogs? Three?! Well, never mind. And the cheesecake was very good; I don't blame you for having second helpings. Besides, you have to enjoy yourself sometimes, don't you.

Sample dialogue (*continued*)

Version 4 (embarrassing silence)
A: Great party, isn't it. I like barbecues, don't you?
B: Mm. [...]
A: I mean, isn't it nice to be outside on summer evenings like this? So warm and ... well, you know. Well, er ... look ... I'm just going to get another hot dot. They are delicious, aren't they? Shall I bring one for you, too?
B: [...]
A: No? Er ... well, no. I don't suppose you're very hungry, are you? I mean, since you've had three already, I suppose ... well, I'll just get them ...

Variation 2   Embarrassing silence

Ask students to think back to scenes in films and plays where someone is trying hard to make conversation with a silent character, e.g., a cool and disinterested lady or a tough western hero, who does not respond, forcing the first person to keep on chatting nervously to cover the embarrassing silences. The students' task is to prepare a new version of the dialogue like this. Remember, the first speaker may not be naturally talkative but has to talk because he/she gets no response from the other. (See **Sample dialogue**, Version 4).

Link

Consider trying **Turn-taking in conversation (7)** from this section, and **Buying time: fillers (11)** and Variation 1 in **You'll never believe this! (20)** from the Conversational strategies section as a follow-up to this activity.

Teacher's diary

How difficult did students find this activity? And how interesting? Were their performances lifelike? What were the main language difficulties?

9   I'm afraid I can't

Level   Intermediate and advanced

Purpose   Explore how to give responses which are unexpected or
                   less favoured by your conversation partner.

Dialogue type Dialogue containing a number of utterance pairs as
                   described in INPUT 6 below

In this activity

Students change the original dialogue by making one speaker choose a more difficult
response to an offer, invitation, apology, etc., i.e., they turn it down, show reluctance,
refuse to accept, etc.

INPUT 6   Utterance pairs with expected and unexpected response options

First utterance	Expected response	Unexpected response
offer	accept	reject
assessment	agree	disagree
apology	accept	not accept
blame	deny	admit
invitation	accept	refuse
request/order	comply/grant/obey	refuse
self-criticism	disagree	agree
question	answer	refuse to answer

Preparation

1. Go through the dialogue and underline all the utterances which require an immediate
    response + the actual responses given (for a list of typical utterance pairs of this
    kind, see INPUT 6).

2. Decide for each pair whether the response was expected, or whether Speaker B

takes a less common option and gives a response which Speaker A is not expecting or does not like. You might want to make copies of INPUT 6 for your students or write it on the board/OHP.

In class

1. Explain to the students that very often when someone is asked or invited to do something or react somehow, there is an easy response, e.g., when you say 'yes' or do (or say) what is expected, and a difficult response, e.g., when you decide to do something which you know the other person will not really like or expect. These less common responses are difficult even for native speakers, let alone foreign language learners, so they need special attention and practice. Show students INPUT 6.

> NOTE: *In some cultures all unexpected or negative responses are unacceptable, therefore students coming from these cultures may need more practice.*

2. Illustrate your point by inviting students to do something ridiculous, e.g., conversation practice at 4 a.m. the next morning, and getting them to refuse politely.

3. Make sure students realise that the difficult or unexpected answers are linguistically more complex. For example, if you accept an invitation, you can say as little as *'Thank you very much, that would be lovely'*, whereas to refuse an invitation you would have to say something like *'Well . . . er . . . I'm awfully sorry but I'm afraid I can't make it on Saturday evening; you see, my niece is arriving from Barcelona and I have promised to meet her at the airport . . . '* (see INPUT 7).

INPUT 7   Typical features of difficult or unexpected responses

1. Start with fillers or hesitation devices
   Oh, er . . . , well, you see, as a matter of fact, actually . . .

2. Start with an apology
   I'm sorry but . . . , I'm afraid I can't . . .

3. Start by seeming to agree
   You're quite right, but . . . ; I know it would be a good time to do it, but . . .

4. End with an explanation or justification
   We've already been invited somewhere else that evening; I promised my mother that I wouldn't do that until I am 18 . . .

---

4. Go through the dialogue with the students, stopping at the parts where there are requests, apologies, etc. and asking them to decide whether the responses given are expected, or less common and therefore difficult ones.

5. In pairs, students rewrite the original dialogue by turning all the expected responses into unexpected or less common ones. In order to keep the sense of the original dialogue, Speaker A should then repeat the question, offer, invitation, etc. more forcefully or give an alternative time, place, etc., and in the end Speaker B should produce the expected response so that the conversation can go on (see **Sample dialogue**).

Sample dialogue

Original

A: I'd love a cup of coffee. Would you make some please, Andrew?
B: Yes, sure. Just a minute, I'll just wash this paint off my hands first.

New version

A: I'd love a cup of coffee. Would you make some please, Andrew?
B: Well ... I'd like to, but I'm afraid there's paint all over my hands
. . .
A: Well, you can wash it off, can't you? *Please*, I'd really appreciate it.
B: Oh, alright. Just a minute, I'll go and wash my hands then ...

---

6. Students perform the new, longer versions of the dialogue.

Follow-up options

1. Ask the students to perform their new versions of the dialogue without looking at their notes or the written text. They should pay special attention to acting out the pauses and hesitation breaks before the difficult responses. Facial expressions and gestures play an important role, too.

2. Discuss which unexpected or less common responses are particularly difficult. Get students to select the two most difficult ones, e.g., by taking a vote. At home, each student should collect three different ways of giving these responses; encourage them to choose solutions which suit their own personality.

3. Students get into pairs. Each pair prepares two versions of a short role-play sketch

based on one of the utterance pairs in INPUT 6. One version should show an expected response and the other an unexpected one.

Variation 1   Reversed responses

Students go through the dialogue noting what kind of responses are given to requests, invitations, etc., i.e., the expected ones or the unexpected and difficult ones. Their job is to reverse these each time; i.e., if a character refuses an invitation in the dialogue, they should accept it in the new version and vice versa. This will mean making quite big changes to the rest of the dialogue so that it follows some sort of logical progression (see **Sample dialogue**).

Sample dialogue

Original

A: Thanks for the coffee. Would you like a cigarette?
B: No thanks, I don't smoke. They're very bad for you, you know.
A: Yes, you're quite right, but I can't give up. I'm a bit pathetic, aren't I?
B: No, of course not! It's very difficult to give up.

New version

A: Thanks for the coffee. Would you like a cigarette?
B: Oh yes please, I'd love one . . . although they're very bad for you, you know.
A: Well, I don't know . . . How can something you enjoy be bad for you? Now that I'm pregnant I do try to smoke less, but I can't give up completely. I'm a bit pathetic, aren't I?
B: Well, I wouldn't say that . . . but perhaps you should think of the baby a bit . . .

Link

Consider trying **Questions and answers (22)** and **How to disagree politely (24)** from the Functions and meanings in conversation section, and **Let's not be so polite (32)** from the Social and cultural contexts section as a follow-up to this activity.

Teacher's diary

Which of the unexpected responses did students think were most difficult to carry out? Can you think of ways of giving students practice in these? Are refusals, disagreements, etc., acceptable in the students' own cultures?

10   It was nice talking to you

Level   Elementary and above

Purpose   Provide a repertoire of phrases to bring a conversation to a
                  close

Dialogue type Any dialogue with two speakers

In this activity

Students rewrite the dialogue in such a way that one speaker refuses to end the
conversation in spite of the efforts of the other.

Preparation

Look at the list of various conversation-closing phrases in INPUT 8. Select about
ten for your students.

In class

1.   Ask students to imagine that they are trapped in conversation with a neighbour
     and they are in a hurry to leave. What phrases can they use to end the conversation
     quickly and politely? Put their ideas on the board/OHP along with those you
     collected previously.

2.   Supposing the neighbour ignores or misunderstands your closing signals? How
     irritating! Tell them to imagine that one speaker in the dialogue is the kind of
     person who will not stop talking, and they must rewrite the dialogue accordingly.
     This will mean extending it and inserting extra closing phrases in the other speaker's
     part.

3.   In pairs, students work on the extension of the dialogue. You may decide to set
     some concrete objectives, e.g., at least three different closing phrases must be
     included.

4.   The pairs perform their versions of the dialogue showing different attempts to
     bring the conversation to a close.

INPUT 8   Bringing a conversation to a close
(Usually a combination of more than one of these phrases is used.)

OK, then ... / Right ... / So ...
Well, I suppose ... / Well, anyway ...
I hope you don't mind, but ...
Would you excuse me, please ...

I've got to go now / I've got to be going now.
I (really) must go / must be going / must be off now.
(Right/well) I should / I'd better be going/moving/getting on my way.
I guess I ought to get back.
(I) must get back to work.
I'm (awfully) sorry, but I'm meeting someone in five minutes / I've got
   to make a phone call.

I'd better let you go.
I'd better not take up any more of your time.

Thanks for your time.
(Once again,) thank you very much (for ... — whatever the other
   speaker said, did or promised to do).
It's been (very) nice/interesting talking to you.

We'll have to get together (again) some time.
(Well anyway,) keep in touch. / Keep me posted (about ...).
Let me know how you get on.
So I'll see you soon/next week.
See you sometime soon, I hope.

I hope everything goes well.
Look after yourself.
Take care.

Follow-up options

1. The students watching the performances could count how many times each structure
    occurs in the performances in order to see which is the class's most popular phrase.
    Of course, they should count their own group's results into the score, too!

2. Another way of bringing a conversation to a close is to conclude it with a proverb or a platitude. Introduce some from INPUT 9 and ask students to incorporate one or two into their performance. This can actually be a game: students should overdo the closings by trying to include as many closing phrases as they can so that the first speaker sounds just as irritating as the one who will not end the conversation!

INPUT 9   Proverbs and platitudes which can be used to conclude a conversation

That's life / (just) the way it goes / the way of the world.
Things always work out for the best.
Makes you think, doesn't it?
It just shows you (you can't be too careful / you never can tell)
You never can tell (you see).
Let's wait and see.
Doesn't time fly?
It happens to the best of us/to us all / It comes to us all.
You've got to take the rough with the smooth.
You can't please everyone.
You can't win them all.
You can't have everything.
Every cloud has a silver lining.
Whatever next, eh?
It'll all turn out for the best.
What would I do without you?

Variation 1   Telephone closings

In telephone conversations you can use many of the closing phrases used in face-to-face talk, but there are also some telephone-specific expressions (see INPUT 10). Ask your students to turn the dialogue into a telephone conversation, then extend it along the lines of the activity above, that is, one person wanting and trying to close the conversation and the other not realising this or deliberately keeping the conversation going!

INPUT 10   Closing phrases for telephone conversations

Listen. I can't talk now.
Someone's just come in.

Someone wants to speak to me.
There's someone on the other line.
I've got some people here (right now).
There are dinner guests here.
Hang on, I can hear something boiling over.
I can hear the doorbell.

Can				
Could	: ring	:		: later.
May I	: call	: you back	: in a few minutes.
I wonder if I could	: phone	:		: when I have more time.

I'll have to go.
Well, I'd better let you go.
Well, I don't want to use/run up your phone bill.

Well, thanks for calling/returning my call.
I'm really glad you called.
I appreciate your calling / It was nice of you to call.
I'll get back to you on that.
Talk to you later.
Well, it's been good talking to you.

Variation 2   Can't say goodbye

In Woody Allen's famous film, *Annie Hall*, there is a scene where the hero and heroine meet for the first time in a doorway, and since they are both shy but rather like each other, neither of them can say goodbye! They keep exchanging closing phrases without actually closing. Ask your students to design and perform a mini-sketch like this, entitled, *Can't Say Goodbye*.

Link

Consider trying Variation 2 of **Relax and chat (1)**, **I haven't got all day! (4)** and Variation 2 of **I couldn't get a word in edgeways (8)** from this section as a follow-up to this activity.

Teacher's diary

Did this activity help students to get the feel of ending conversations? Did they sound natural when doing so? Can you think of other ways of facilitating this skill?

SECTION II

CONVERSATIONAL STRATEGIES

Introduction

Conversational strategies are the invaluable means of remaining in control of the conversation when communication difficulties arise, and they also enhance the efficiency of communication. Knowing such strategies is particularly useful for language learners since they provide them with a sense of security in the language by allowing them extra time and room to manoeuvre. The following is a brief description of the most important conversational strategies and techniques with indications of the activities in the chapter which focuses on them.

One common source of communication breakdown is when one cannot remember or does not know a word or expression. This happens sometimes in our mother tongue as well, and at such times native speakers tyically call into action one or more of the following strategies.

Message adjustment or avoidance

This involves tailoring your message to your competence, i.e., saying what you can say rather than what you want to say. This can be done either through making a slight alteration or reduction of the message, or even by avoiding it completely (**19 Going off the point**).

Paraphrasing

This involves describing or exemplifying the object or action whose name you do not know (**17 The thing you open bottles with**).

Using approximation

This means using an alternative term which expresses the meaning of the target word as closely as possible, e.g., *ship* for *sailing boat* (**17 The thing you open bottles with**).

Mime

(Variation 1 in **18 What do you call it?**).

Appeal for help

This includes eliciting the word you are looking for from your communication partner by asking questions like 'What's the word for ... ? (**18 What do you call it?**).

Other trouble spots in communication, including misunderstandings and comprehension problems, can be sorted out by what linguists call *repair*; this involves asking questions to check and ensure understanding, as well as correcting what one or the other speaker has said. Examples of repair in this section are:

Asking the other speaker to repeat when you have not heard or understood something (**12 Pardon?**).

Asking the other speaker to explain something you do not understand (**13 What do you mean?**).

Checking whether the other person has understood what you have said (**14 Is that clear?**).

Checking whether the other person is paying attention to what you are saying (**15 Are you listening?**).

Reformulating what you or the other speaker have said (**16 In other words**).

A general conversational strategy which can be used to gain time to think when any communication difficulty occurs, or when something takes you by surprise, is the use of *fillers* or *hesitation devices* (**11 Buying time: fillers**).

To conclude this section there is an activity which focuses on narrative story-telling techniques; these can be used in conversation to hold the listener's attention by making what you say sound more interesting or dramatic (**20 You'll never believe this!**).

11   Buying time: fillers

Level   Elementary and above

Purpose   Develop strategies to gain time in conversation by using
                   fillers and hesitation devices

Dialogue type Any dialogue

In this activity

Students prepare a new version of the dialogue, in which speakers delay their answers
by using fillers and hesitation devices.

Preparation

1. Make a list of some fillers or hesitation devices you would like to introduce to
    your students (see INPUT 11).

INPUT 11   Common fillers and hesitation devices
(Very often a combination of several fillers is used.)

Well . . .	The thing is . . .
Um . . ./er . . .	I see what you mean.
Actually . . .	Sort of.
You know/see . . .	That sort/kind of thing.
I see.	It's like this, you see . . .
I/you mean . . .	Right then.
As a matter of fact . . .	Let's say . . .
Let's see (now).	What I'm trying to say is . . .
Now let me think/see.	(Now) where should I start . . .
I'll have to think about it.	That's a good/very interesting question.
Frankly, . . .	What I would say is . . .
To be (quite) honest/frank, . . .	How shall I put it.
In fact, . . .	Let's put it this way . . .
I wonder . . .	The best way I can answer that is . . .
Hang on.	I('ll) tell you what . . .

---

2. Collect some questions you cannot expect anybody to know the answers to, e.g., *'Who won the 100 metre sprint at the 1912 Olympic Games?'* or *'What is the fourth biggest city in Siberia?'*, etc.

In class

1. Begin by asking students questions such as, *'What were you doing last Friday at 11.15 am?'* or *'Where did you spend the summer seven years ago?'* They are unlikely to be able to answer immediately and will probably stammer, laugh, lapse into silence or say *'I don't know'*.

2. One way to react to difficult questions is to use certain filling words or phrases to gain some time to think. Demonstrate this by answering one of your own difficult questions using several fillers. Ask someone what fillers they know, and list them on the board/OHP along the ones you have selected.

3. Get the students to ask each other difficult questions so that they can practise using fillers. Point out that a combination of several fillers sounds more like a native speaker and gives them even more time to think! For example:
   Question: *Why haven't you done your homework?*
   Answer: *Well ... er, you see, it's like this ... now, where shall I start ... ? etc.*

4. Students get into pairs/groups and prepare a version of the dialogue in which all the speakers are terribly uncertain and hesitant and use lots of fillers.

5. Students perform the new versions of the dialogue and the audience notes all the different fillers that were used. Which were the most popular?

Follow-up options

1. Ask students to perform the hesitant version of the dialogue again, but this time every student should have a favourite filler which they use more often than any other. The students watching the performances spot what the favourite filler of each of the performers is.

2. Play some authentic cassette or video recording to the class and ask them to write down all the different fillers they hear, and also to count how many times each filler appears. They should hear the text at least twice for this activity.

3. In pairs or groups, or individually at home, students extend a dialogue as much as they can by adding only fillers to it.

Variation 1   How embarrassing!

Prepare cue cards containing embarrassing situations, such as

> there is a hole in one of the speakers' trousers,
> one of the speakers' flies are open,
> someone has got a jumper on inside out,
> someone has trodden in something revolting,
> there is a mark on one of the speakers' shirt, blouse, etc.

Hand out one card to each group and ask students to prepare a version of the dialogue where one speaker notices the embarrassing element, tries to call the other's attention to it, but being too embarrassed he/she does not come straight to the point but hesitates, using fillers. The other character should be a bit slow to notice what the whole thing is about!

Variation 2   Unexpected questions

Students perform the original dialogue but insert extra embarrassing or difficult questions into it. These could be written on cue cards and given to the students, or students could invent their own. The main thing is that the other character is not expecting the question and therefore uses fillers to gain time to think of an answer.

Link

Consider trying Variation 2 of **I couldn't get a word in edgeways (8)** and Variation 2 of **It was nice talking to you (10)** from the Conversational rules and structure section, and **Going off the point (19)** from this section as a follow-up to this activity.

Teacher's diary

Is there any way you can classify fillers? Can everything go with everything else? Were students using the fillers appropriately? Did they see how fillers can be useful? Do you think it is worth having them to do this activity again in the future to remind them to use fillers?

---

12 Pardon?

Level	Elementary and above
Purpose	Develop strategies to ask for repetition in order to clarify meaning
Dialogue type	Any dialogue with two speakers

In this activity

Students perform the dialogue pretending they do not understand or did not hear certain things and ask the other speaker to repeat.

Preparation

Make a list of phrases that can be used to ask someone to repeat something when you do not understand. Include some your students already know and add some new ones (see INPUT 12).

In class

1. When you go into class, start talking very quietly and very fast so that students cannot understand you. Do any of them manage to ask you in English to repeat? Discuss different phrases they could use in situations like this, and put these on the board/OHP.

2. Students get into pairs. Tell them that their task will be to extend the dialogue by imagining that the speakers have to keep asking each other to repeat things, either because they are in a noisy place or because they have difficulty understanding each other. Encourage them not to speak clearly but mutter in order to make the situation more realistic.

3. Each pair is to choose four phrases from the list on the board (two for each student) and write these phrases (and the other speaker's repetitions) into the conversation.

4. The pairs perform the extended conversations.

INPUT 12 Asking for repetition

(I'm) sorry? / (I) (beg your) pardon?

(I'm) sorry, I didn't	: hear : catch : get : understand	: : : :	the	: last part. : part about ... : last/first word.

Sorry, what did you say? / what was that again?

What was that word/the first word/his name/the last sentence again?

Would/Could you repeat that/what you said/that name/the last word, please?

Could you repeat that for me, please?

Would you mind repeating that?

Sorry, can/could you say that again please?

Sorry, can/could you repeat it more slowly?

Sorry, would you mind speaking a bit slower?

I'm sorry, I couldn't/didn't hear (what you said).

I'm sorry, when/who/where/what time did you say?

Sorry, did you say 'Nottingham'?

What? / You what? / When? / Where? / Who? / What kind of ... ?

Hang on/Just a minute, say that again / I didn't quite catch that.

Follow-up options

1. Taking the situation to the extreme, students perform the dialogue (this time without looking at their notes) pretending that two slightly deaf people are talking, which makes understanding each other almost hopeless. Encourage them to gradually raise their voices.

2. To make the situation more lifelike, you may put on some loud background music which really would make understanding difficult!

3. Chain misunderstanding: Students sit in a circle; S1 turns to S2 and says something, e.g., *'Grandpa was there last night'*; S2 doesn't understand this and asks S1 to repeat; S1 repeats the sentence, S2 acknowledges it, then turns to S3 and repeats a distorted version of the sentence, e.g., *'Grandma is coming tonight'*. S3 asks back, then repeats to S4 another distorted version, e.g., *'Andrew's car is all right'*, etc. If the class is in a creative mood, some students can ask more than one question before the final misunderstanding; for example:

    S1: *A man with a red hat is coming.*
    S2: *Sorry, what was that again?*

S1: (louder) *A man with a red hat is coming.*
S2: *What kind of hat?*
S1: *Red.*
S2: *Did you say dead?*
S1: *No, I said R E D !!*
S2: *Oh, I see.* (to S3) *A woman with a dead cat is coming ...*

Variation 1   I'm sorry, the line is very bad

For this activity you can either select a special dialogue which is a telephone conversation, or you can use the same dialogue as before and get students, as a first task, to turn it into a telephone conversation.

On the telephone it is easy to misunderstand or not understand someone because you cannot see him/her, and sometimes the line is bad or the phone is in a noisy place. In many cases you can use the same phrases to ask for repetition as in a face-to-face conversation (see INPUT 12), but there are some expressions especially for telephone talk (see INPUT 13). Introduce these, then get students (in pairs) to extend the telephone conversation by imagining that the line is very bad and the speakers have to keep asking each other to repeat things.

Again you could put on loud background music or have the students sit back to back in order to make the situation more lifelike.

INPUT 13   Asking for repetition on the phone

I'm sorry, the line's very bad ...
Could you speak up (a bit), please (I can't hear you over the noise here).

(I'm) sorry (but)		hear	that.
Excuse me, (but)	I didn't	get	what you said.
I'm afraid		understand	

Could/Can/Would you repeat that (for me), please?
Would you mind repeating that?
Excuse me, could you repeat more slowly / could you say that more slowly?
Sorry, did you say 'Nottingham'?
Could you spell that, please?
Sorry, I didn't get any of that.
What was that again?
Sorry, can/could you say that again, please?
Hang on/just a minute, I didn't quite catch that.

Link

Consider trying **What do you mean? (13), In other words (16)** and **What do you call it? (18)** from this section as a follow-up to this activity.

Teacher's diary

Is asking for repetition covered and practised in enough detail in the teaching material you use? Is there the same variety of ways of asking for repetition in the students' native language as there is in English? Did students notice any differences in the politeness and formality of the phrases?

---

13   What do you mean?

Level   Elementary and above

Purpose   Provide practice in asking for explanations

Dialogue type Any dialogue with two speakers

In this activity

Students introduce some difficult words and phrases into the dialogue so that their
conversation partner has to ask for explanations.

INPUT 14   Getting someone to explain something you have not understood

What do you mean? / What do you mean by . . . ?
Do you mean (that) . . . ? / Does that mean (that) . . . ?
What exactly does that mean?
What are you saying/trying to say?
Don't you mean . . . ?
What (exactly) does . . . mean?

Could/Would you explain this word, please?
'Trade convention'?/'Curriculum'?/etc. (echoing the problem word with
  a question intonation).

Sorry, I didn't understand (the word) . . .
Sorry, I'm lost. / I'm afraid you've lost me there.
Sorry, I don't/didn't quite follow you/what you were saying about . . .
I'm not sure I understand/follow you.
I'm afraid I don't understand.
I don't quite see what you mean/what you're getting at, I'm afraid.
I'm sorry, I'm not quite clear on . . .
I don't get you/it/the point.

Preparation

1. Make up a list of questions and phrases which people use when they have not understood what their conversation partner said (see INPUT 14).

2. Look through the dialogue you will be using in class, pick out two words or phrases for each speaker (A and B) and write difficult or more complicated versions of these on two separate cue cards (one for A and one for B). For example:

```
                        Speaker A

   Lots of traffic  =  an abundance of vehicles
   fish             =  mackerel
```

Make enough copies of each card for half of the class.

3. Write speaker A's part of the dialogue on a separate sheet from Speaker B's (i.e., make two dialogue halves) and, again, make enough copies for everybody to have one of the dialogue halves.

In class

1. To start with, turn to a student and say something which includes a very difficult or even an imaginary word. Can the student ask you in English to explain the word (and not just repeat it)? If not, try another student. This should lead to a discussion of different ways of asking for explanations. Make a list of these on the board/OHP.

2. Practise using these phrases by saying one or two difficult sentences and getting students to ask for an explanation; when they do, you reformulate the sentence in simpler language.

3. Students get into pairs. Hand out the dialogue halves (a Part A and a Part B to each pair) and give them time to look over their own part.

4. Hand out the cue cards. Using the dialogue halves, students perform the dialogue, but they must say the difficult word or phrase on their cue card instead of the original and simpler version. When the other speaker hears a difficult part, he/she should ask for an explanation, using the phrases learnt (see **Sample dialogue** below).

5. After students have had some practice, get one or two pairs to volunteer to perform the dialogue for the class, but this time the speakers should include imaginary words (instead of difficult ones) to elicit requests for explanation.

Sample dialogue

Original

A: There's lots of traffic on this road today, isn't there?
B: Yes, it's because they're doing some repair work on King's Road.

New version

A: There's an abundance of vehicles on this road today, isn't there?
B: Sorry, I'm afraid I don't understand ...
A: There's lots of traffic.
B: Oh, yes. That's because road works are in progress on King's Road.
A: Sorry, what do you mean by 'road works are in progress'?

Follow-up options

1. Taking the original dialogue, i.e., the version without the difficult bits, students in pairs pretend they are both a bit 'slow' and keep having to ask for explanation because they do not understand something. It then has to be reformulated by the other speaker. For example:

   A: *They'll be arriving tomorrow morning.*
   B: *What do you mean?*
   A: *I mean they're coming here tomorrow before lunch.*

2. You may turn the performances into a game by asking the listeners to count which question structure each pair used and how many times each. This will involve the other students who might otherwise passively watch the performances.

Variation 1   Three difficult words

Ask students to bring in dictionaries. Hand out the dialogue halves as you did in the previous activity, but this time each student must write into their parts three difficult words from dictionary (which, of course, they have to be able to explain simply!). The other speaker will probably have to ask for these words to be explained.

Variation 2   Sorry, I'm a language learner

Explain to the students that asking for explanation is common in one's mother tongue, but particularly useful for a language learner as he/she can use this strategy to control the conversation. Ask them to change one of the roles in the original dialogue so that the speaker is a language learner who is very uncertain and wants to doublecheck all the time whether he/she has understood everything correctly.

Link

Consider trying **Pardon? (12)** and **In other words (16)** from this section as a follow-up to this activity.

Teacher's diary

Is it acceptable in your students' own culture to ask questions like those practised in the activities above? If not, how do they indicate that they do not understand something? Which phrases did students find most useful?

---

14   Is that clear?

Level   Elementary and above

Purpose   Practise asking questions to check whether the other
                     understands

Dialogue type   Dialogue with explanation, instructions or narration

In this activity

Students add check questions to the dialogue where one speaker is not sure whether
the other is following and understanding.

Preparation

1. List check questions you would like to teach to your students (see INPUT 15).

INPUT 15   Questions to check whether the other understands what you are saying and possible responses

Check questions	Responses
OK? / Right?	Mmm . . . / Uh-huh.
Is that clear?	(Yes,) sure.
Are you with me?	Oh yes, go on.
Do/Can you follow me?	Of course.
All right/OK so far?	Yes, get on with it!
Got/Get it (so far)?	More or less, yes.
Do you see what I mean / what I'm getting at?	Sort of . . .
. . . if you see what I mean / follow me	Well, not really . . .
Am I making / Have I made myself clear?	Er . . .
Does that make sense (to you)?	Well . . .
Am I making sense?	
Do I make myself clear/understood?	
Do you understand (me)?	

---

2. Look through the dialogue and mark places where one speaker could logically ask check questions.

In class

1. The best thing to do when you are not sure whether your partner can follow what you are saying is to ask them. Elicit from students some questions you could ask in such situations, put them on the board/OHP, and add the ones you have collected. You could demonstrate your point by giving a short but complicated explanation, e.g., of directions, first without and then with check questions. Discuss also what the response to such check questions could be (see INPUT 15).

2. Tell the students they are going to make one (or more) of the speakers in the dialogue add some check questions where they think they might be needed. You could suggest the places you marked.

3. In pairs or threes (depending on the number of characters) students insert check questions into the dialogue. Some responses could be negative so that the speaker has to repeat or simplify what he/she has said (see INPUT 17).

4. Students read out or perform the extended versions. The others count how many question structures each group used.

Follow-up options

1. This time, students might add lots more check questions where they are not needed so that the second speaker starts to get really irritated. He/she should show this impatience in his/her voice and finally say something like *'Get on with it!'* or *'I'm not stupid!'* as a response.

2. At home, students prepare a little explanation or set of instructions of their own which must contain some information that other students would not know, e.g., a cookery recipe, how to rebuild or put together something or how to get to your favourite pub from the zoo. In pairs, they explain these things to each other, regularly asking check questions. It is important that the other student understands every step, because he/she will have to write a brief summary for homework — or perhaps explain the same thing to another student!

Variation 1   Do I make myself understood?!

Strangely enough, some of the check questions mentioned above are also used as warnings or threats by people who are angry with someone. For example:

> (Teacher to pupil:) *If I see you throwing paper again, you'll be going to the headmistress' office. Is that clear?*

(Girlfriend to boyfriend:) *I can't stand the way you treat me. I won't put up with it! Do you understand me?*

(Boss to employee:) *If your work doesn't improve I'm going to have to take unpopular action. Do you follow me?*

Decide with students which of the questions on the sample list are good for this purpose. Then, in pairs, students rewrite the dialogue so that one speaker is angry with the other (they invent the reason) and makes some threats like these above.

Link

Consider trying **Are you listening? (15)** from this section, and **Reactions (25)** from the Functions and meanings in conversation section as a follow-up to this activity.

Teacher's diary

Did students find it easy to include check questions in the dialogue? Do they often ask such questions in their mother tongue?

---

15   Are you listening?

Level   Elementary and above

Purpose   Develop ways of checking whether your conversation
                   partner is paying attention

Dialogue type Any dialogue with two speakers

In this activity

Students act out the dialogue: Student B is obviously not listening so an irritated Student
A must keep asking 'attention-regaining' questions.

Preparation

1.   Prepare a list of four or five phrases your students can use when they want to
     check during conversation if their conversation partner is listening (see INPUT 16).

INPUT 16   Checking that the other is listening

Are you listening?
Did you hear what I said?
Am I boring you?
You are not listening, are you?
What do you think?
Do you agree?
Are you all right? / Is there anything wrong?
I can tell you're extremely interested in what I'm saying! (sarcastically)

(To be more polite, you can ask questions like those in INPUT 15.)

On the phone

Hello? Hello?
Are you (still) there?
Can you hear me?

---

2. Go through the dialogue you will be using in class and mark some places where Speaker B's attention could drift away forcing Speaker A to ask an 'attention-regaining' question. Some places are after a question by Speaker A (Speaker B does not answer immediately) or at a point where Speaker B could miss a reaction.

In class

1. Ask two volunteers to come to the front of the class and discuss a programme they saw the previous night on television. One should be really enthusiastic and keen to talk, the other uninterested and unresponsive. Ask the class how the enthusiastic one probably feels: Upset? Irritated? Both?

2. Brainstorm ways of checking whether the other person is listening and ways of regaining their attention. Write these and your list on the board. Explain that some are not very polite and should only be used with people you know quite well.

3. Discuss what the other speaker's reaction might be to these questions. This is usually an apology, insistence that he/she *was* listening, reassurance that Speaker A is *not* boring, etc.

4. Students get into pairs and rewrite the dialogue so that Speaker A must constantly check whether Speaker B is listening. Point out the places you have marked where Speaker B could fail to respond. Ask students to use at least three different 'attention-regaining' questions, starting politely at first and then getting less polite. The end of the new dialogue might be different from the textbook ending!

5. Students perform the new version of the dialogue. Did any group manage to avoid a conflict between their characters?

Follow-up options

1. Put as many 'attention-regaining' questions as you can on the board. Ask the students to divide them into two categories: ones that can be used by (a) good friends with each other, and (b) acquaintances with each other. Discuss the results; note that some phrases can fall into both categories.

2. Ask students to consider the reasons any Speaker B might have for not listening to Speaker A. Collect these on the blackboard under two headings, (a) those that are completely unacceptable and make Speaker A angry and upset, e.g., Speaker B finds Speaker A boring, and (b) those which are more acceptable, e.g., Speaker B has serious problems.

Variation 1   Are you still there?

On the telephone a missing reaction from the other speaker can be even more disturbing than in face-to-face conversation, although it might well happen because Speaker B cannot hear rather than because he/she is not listening. See INPUT 16 for phrases one might say in such cases. Ask students to turn the dialogue into a telephone conversation with Speaker A having to check constantly whether Speaker B is still there. Once again, the end could be angry! You can also combine these phrases with those in INPUT 13 expressing 'requests for repetition on the phone'.

Link

Consider trying **Pardon? (12)** and **Is that clear? (14)** from this section, and **Reactions (25)** from the Functions and meanings in conversation section as a follow-up to this activity.

Teacher's diary

How is this quite delicate situation handled in the students' own language/culture? Are 'attention-regaining' questions acceptable? Did they find asking such questions on the phone more natural? Why (not)?

---

16   In other words

Level   Advanced

Purpose   Explore how to (a) reformulate your message if it has not
                   been understood, and (b) rephrase the other person's words
                   to check your understanding of them

Dialogue type Any two-speaker dialogue which contains some
                   explanations or arguments

In this activity

Students extend the dialogue by making one speaker interpret wrongly what the other
has said, forcing the other to reformulate his/her message.

Preparation

1. Make two lists of starting phrases: (a) phrases to interpret or reformulate the other's
    message if you are not sure you have understood it, and (b) phrases to reformulate
    your message when the other has not understood (see INPUT 17).

2. Prepare a short dialogue (see **Sample dialogue**, Original version) in which the
    two speakers use these strategies to clarify meaning.

In class

1. Ask a student to explain to you how they come to school, college, etc. At some
    point you should look puzzled. Then repeat what you have heard in your own
    words and deliberately misunderstand something. This will cause the student to
    explain the route again in different words.

2. Point out that the misunderstanding here was sorted out by reformulating the
    message (twice!). Present your two lists of starting phrases which can be used
    in such cases.

INPUT 17   Saying things in other words

Interpreting or reformulating what the other speaker has said

If I('ve) understood you correctly/right . . .
You mean (then) . . . (right?) / Do you mean to say . . . ? / So you mean . . . ?
Do you mean . . .? / Does that mean?
What you mean (to say) is . . . / What you're saying/trying to say is . . .
Are you saying that . . . ? / So you are saying . . .
In other words . . .
If I've got it right, (then) . . .
If I follow you rightly, then . . .
So am I right in saying that . . .
So the basic/general idea is that . . .

Reformulating what you said: when the listener has not understood

That's not quite/exactly it/what I meant (to say) . . .
That's not really what I'm/I was getting at . . .
It's not actually/quite that simple/complicated . . .
There's more to it than that . . .
It's really more a case/question of . . .
What I said was . . .
What I really meant/mean was/is . . .
What I'm really saying/trying to say is . . .
Basically, what I meant was . . .
Sorry, let me explain it more clearly/in another way/better . . .
Let me put it in another way . . .
In other words . . . / That is to say . . . (only without interruption from other
   speaker)

When the listener misunderstood you and started to get upset

(No,) don't get me wrong, (what I meant (to say) was) . . .
(No,) don't misunderstand me . . .
You must have misunderstood me . . .
(No,) I didn't mean that . . .
That's not what I said/meant (to say) . . .
All I was trying to say is . . .

3. The students' task is to prepare a new version of the dialogue in which one speaker does not understand things, forcing the other speaker to do some reexplanation (see **Sample dialogue**, Version 1). To make it more realistic, you may encourage them to first make the original explanations in the dialogue more complicated.

Sample dialogue

Original

Molly: So before we go to Auntie Carol's, let's have a drink at Uncle Bill's, and when my Dad comes, we'll go and join the rest of the family and eat. OK?

Tim: Yes, that sounds great.

Version 1

Molly: So before we go to Auntie Carol's, let's have a drink at Uncle Bill's, and when my Dad comes, we'll go and join the rest of the family and eat. OK?

Tim: So, if I've got it right, we go to the pub with Uncle Bill and your Dad, then we go and meet your family and later the two of us go to a restaurant?

Molly: Er . . . no, that's not quite what I meant . . . Let me explain it more clearly: First we'll have a drink at Uncle Bill's house . . . etc.

---

4. In pairs, students write then perform their extended versions of the dialogue.

Follow-up option

Ask the students to act out an exaggerated, comedy-like version of the extended dialogue, in which one speaker is so slow that in spite of all the explanations he/she simply does not get the point.

Variation 1   Don't get me wrong!

This time students concentrate on *misunderstanding*. Speaker B (Tim) can follow Speaker A (Molly) but sees another meaning in her words. Molly is forced to reformulate her point, using expressions such as those listed at the end of INPUT 17 to reassure him (see **Sample dialogue**, Version 2). Students rewrite the dialogue along these lines.

Sample dialogue

Version 2 (misunderstanding)

Molly: So before we go to Auntie Carol's, let's have a drink at Uncle
         Bill's, and when my Dad comes, we'll go and join the rest of
         the family and eat. OK?

Tim: So what you're saying is that we're going to spend the whole of
         Saturday night with your family because you don't want to be
         alone with me?

Molly: Oh, Tim, don't misunderstand me! It's not the whole night! We
         can leave before ten o'clock. It's just that it's my Mum's
         birthday.

Link

Consider trying **What do you mean? (13)** from this section, and **Change without
changing (26)** and **Paranoia or a hidden meaning in everything (28)** from
the Functions and meanings in conversation section as a follow-up to this activity.

Teacher's diary

How did the students do in this activity? Did some of them find the
reformulating task too difficult? Can you think of any other ways of
practising reformulating skills? Are they covered in any detail in the
coursebook(s) you use?

17 The thing you open bottles with

Level   Elementary and above

Purpose   Provide training in the use of paraphrase and approximation (= using an alternative word)

Dialogue type   Any dialogue with two speakers

In this activity

While acting out the dialogue, students are not allowed to say certain key words and must overcome this difficulty with paraphrase and approximation, i.e., using an alternative word.

Preparation

1. Choose a dialogue which the students know, and pick out some content words (nouns, verbs, adjectives or adverbs) which have a key function in the conversation, and which do not have obvious synonyms.

2. Prepare a skeleton of the dialogue, that is, select one or two important words from each sentence that can remind the students of how the conversation goes, and put these on the board/OHP. For example, *'It's lovely to see you again!'* can be abbreviated to *... lovely ... see ... .* Alternatively, you could use some other 'memory hooks' like drawings, visual aids, etc.

In class

1. Discuss with the class what people can do when they have forgotten or do not know an important word. Introduce the following two useful strategies:

    Paraphrase, i.e., describing or exemplifying the object or action whose name you do not know, e.g., 'the thing you open bottles with' for 'corkscrew'.
    Approximation, i.e., using a word which expresses the meaning of the target word as closely as possible, e.g., 'ship' for 'sailing boat'.

2. Teach the students some useful structures for paraphrase (see INPUT 18), and get them to practise these by paraphrasing a number of easy nouns for someone else to guess the word.

INPUT 18   Useful structures for paraphrase

a kind/sort of . . . / it's a kind/sort of . . .
something which you (can) . . . (with).
the thing you use for . . .
the thing you can . . . (with).
it's what you . . . (with).
someone/the person who . . .
it's a bit like . . .
it's when you . . .
you do/say it when. . .
it's something/the kind of thing you do/say when . . .

3. Give students some time to look over the dialogue, then ask them to cover up the text and perform it in pairs looking only at the dialogue skeleton you have written on the board.

4. Tell students they are going to act out the dialogue without saying some key words — they will have to pretend that they cannot remember these words and use the paraphrase and approximation strategies they have learnt.

5. Write on the board the words students must not say (one for each speaker in the dialogue). In pairs, students perform the dialogue using the strategies discussed. After they have had one go, replace the key words with another two.

Follow-up options

1. When you change the key words at Stage 5, do not wipe off the previous two, and students then do the task with four missing words (two each). Keep adding to the list, and see how many words the students can manage to paraphrase and still keep the sense of the dialogue.

2. Students go through the dialogue replacing all the nouns and verbs, or as many as possible, with approximations! Does the dialogue still make sense?

3. Students think of a word in their own language for which they do not know the English word but would like to! They go round the class paraphrasing or approximating the word for their classmates; perhaps someone else knows the word and can help them! Of course, there must be no mother tongue used, especially in a monolingual class. If no-one can help, they should bring their paraphrase or approximation to you, the teacher.

Variation 1   The paraphrase survey

Students draw up a list of all the paraphrase structures they have learnt, then choose a word from the dialogue which they would like the other students to paraphrase. They go round the class asking others to explain this word as if to someone who does not understand it. Each time the students hear a particular paraphrase structure, they mark it off on their list. The class comes together afterwards and finds out which were the most frequently used strategies.

Link

Consider trying **Buying time: fillers (11)** and **What do you call it? (18)** from this section as a follow-up to this activity.

Teacher's diary

Did students choose to paraphrase words more or less often than giving an approximation of the words? Were some students better at using these strategies than others? What other activities do you know which focus on giving definitions and paraphrasing?

---

18   What do you call it?

Level   Elementary and above

Purpose   Develop strategies to ask for help from a communication
                 partner when in difficulty

Dialogue type Any dialogue with two speakers

In this activity

Students must not mention certain key words in the dialogue but rather elicit them
from the other speaker by appealing for help.

Preparation

1. Collect a list of ways of asking how to say a word (see INPUT 19).

INPUT 19   Appealing for help

What do / would you call it? / someone who ... ? / the thing which ... ?

What's the word for .../to describe (it) ... ?
How do/would you say ... ?
I can't remember / I've forgotten the word for ... ?
What's the name of ... ?

---

2. Select a dialogue your students know, and pick out the most important content
   words (nouns, verbs, adjectives). Write down just these words in order next to
   the name of the character who says them in the dialogue, like this:

   John: *greengrocers   hurrying*
   Ted: *important   doctor*

3. Put this skeleton dialogue on the board/OHP.

In class

1. Ask students what sort of questions they can ask if they have forgotten or do not know a word and cannot think of a synonym. Write their ideas on the board, and add the phrases from your list which they have not said.

2. Get the students into pairs and ask them to look at the skeleton dialogue on the board. Explain that when they perform the dialogue, they must not look at the original text, only at this skeleton. Give them time to go through the text once more and practise reconstructing the dialogue from the skeleton.

3. Now comes the real task. Students act out the dialogue again, with Speaker A pretending not to remember certain words. It is up to them to decide which ones, as long as there is one word from every line of their speech. They therefore have to elicit these words from Speaker B. For example, if the word to avoid is *nurse* in the question, *'Did you tell the nurse?'*, the dialogue may go like this:

    > A: *Did you tell the ... er ... I can't remember the word for the person who takes care of the patients ... What do you call her? ... the woman in white ... What's the word ... ?*
    > B: *Nurse?*
    > A: *That's it! Did you tell the nurse?*

4. After the performance, students should change roles so that the other speaker can have a go at forgetting words!

Follow-up option

Ask the students to act out the dialogue again but this time Speaker B should be a bit slow to understand what the other is getting at, and should come up with wrong words first. For example:

> S1: *Did you tell the ... er ... What do you call the person who takes care of the patients ... ?*
> S2: *Doctor?*
> S1: *No, the woman in white ... ?*
> S2: *Ah, the maid!* etc.

Variation 1   Mime the word

Sometimes when you cannot remember a word, you mime it for the other person. For example:

A: *I would like to* . . . (pretending to iron with his/her hand) . . . *my shirt* . . . *you know* . . . (mime again) . . . *what do you call it?*

B: *Ah, you want to iron your shirt* . . .

In pairs, students perform the dialogue using mime only when they appeal for help and not paraphrase or synonyms.

Link

Consider trying **What do you mean? (13)** and **The thing you open bottles with (17)** from this section as a follow-up to this activity.

Teacher's diary

Did the students learn to use all the question structures you presented? What difficulties did they have during the activity? How else could you practise using these questions more naturally?

---

19 Going off the point

Level   Intermediate and advanced

Purpose   Practise two important communication strategies: adjusting
                   your message and avoiding the topic

Dialogue type Any dialogue

In this activity

Students vary the original dialogue by making one speaker deliberately go off the
point and evade questions

Preparation

1. Take a simple question—answer exchange and rewrite it by making the second
   speaker avoid getting a straightforward answer (see **Sample dialogue 1**).

Sample dialogue 1

Question: How old are you?
Answer: Well, that's an interesting question. Isn't it strange how
           people always feel that they need to know the age of a
           person? I don't really think that age is important at all.

---

2. Collect a list of short, factual questions, e.g., 'What's your name?', 'Have you
   got any brothers and sisters?', 'What country do you come from?' etc.

In class

1. Explain to your students that being able to 'go off the point' can be a very useful
   skill in difficult moments in conversation or at oral language exams! What other
   situations can the students think of where they could use this skill?

2. Present **Sample dialogue 1**, then take one of your factual questions and ask
   everybody to prepare a short speech of four or five sentences to evade the answer.
   They are welcome to take notes. Encourage them to use fillers and hesitation devices
   (see INPUT 11).

71

3. Listen to the speeches, make helpful comments if necessary, then ask further questions which students have to evade, this time without any preparation.

4. Students get into pairs or groups and prepare a new version of the dialogue in which one speaker keeps going off the point and the other speaker(s) must politely remind him/her of what they were talking about (the 'return to the topic' phrases in INPUT 3 may come in useful here) (see **Sample dialogue 2**).

Sample dialogue 2

Original

A: Have you been to the bank to pay that cheque in?
B: No, not yet. I'll go this afternoon.
A: Do you promise?
B: Yes, of course. I won't forget.

Going off the point

A: Have you been to the bank to pay that cheque in?
B: Well, as a matter of fact, I thought I'd go and buy some white paint this afternoon. You know, for the garage door. Do you think it would look-nice white?
A: Charles, I asked you about the bank! Have you been or will you go this afternoon?
B: Well, you know, I'm a busy person but I always have time to do extra things like painting the garage door and mending the fence
 . . .

---

5. The pairs or groups perform their versions.

Follow-up options

1. Prepare cue cards, one for each student, each containing an odd sentence, e.g., *Rhinos are faster than elephants* or *Yesterday's ice cream was delicious*. Students must deviate from the original conversation so that they can include their odd sentence naturally, i.e., so that it does not stand out. The audience must try and spot these odd sentences.

2. Politicians often go off the point. In fact, they very rarely answer questions directly, but rather try and talk about what they have prepared in advance. Organise a press conference in the classroom, where the journalists keep asking the famous politician(s) factual questions, and he/she must try to avoid answering them directly.

Variation 1   Pet subject

Some people have favourite topics and direct the conversation towards these regardless of what they are asked. Students prepare a new version of the dialogue turning one speaker into someone like this. The task is therefore not to avoid answering questions but to steer the conversation to the character's favourite topic. You may suggest a few possible themes, e.g., the immorality of youth, tennis, when I was in . . ., etc., but students may want to invent their own pet subjects. Another idea is for groups to choose topics for the other groups.

Variation 2   Secret agents

Secret agents are, by definition, very secretive; they would never answer a question directly. Ask your students to imagine that all the characters in the dialogue are master spies and the role they are playing is only a disguise. Students must rewrite the dialogue so that it becomes a series of answer evasions on both sides.

Link

Consider trying **By the way, that reminds me (2)** and **I haven't got all day! (4)** from the Conversational rules and structure section, and **Buying time: fillers (11)** from this section as a follow-up to this activity.

> ### Teacher's diary
>
> Were those students who are traditionally recognised as 'good' students, i.e., grammatically competent, gaining good exam results, better at this activity? To what extent is going off the point acceptable in the students' own language?

20 You'll never believe this!

Level   Intermediate and advanced

Purpose   Develop narrative techniques to tell stories and present facts dynamically

Dialogue type   Dialogue with two speakers in which one of them tells a story or relates events

In this activity

Students extend the dialogue by making one speaker use narrative techniques to make his/her part sound more interesting.

Preparation

1. Look at the expressions in INPUT 20. Select the ones you would like to teach to your students, and add further ones you can think of. Write these on the board/OHP.

2. Collect a list of trivial things someone did, e.g., She opened the door, She took off her shoes, She cleaned her teeth, etc.

In class

1. Say two or three of the trivial sentences you have collected in a flat, boring voice, then say them again in a more dramatic way, adding phrases from your list, e.g., *'This is hard to believe, but she cleaned her teeth! Then guess what? She took off her shoes!'*

2. Present the list of phrases and then get the students to try to make trivial sentences sound exciting.

3. Students get into pairs and prepare a new version of the dialogue in which Speaker A uses this dramatic story-telling style with at least three of the new phrases in his/her part. The other character should react by saying, *'Really'*, *'I see'*, *'Interesting'*, etc., without actually showing any interest, thus urging the first speaker to make even greater efforts to be interesting (see **Sample dialogue**).

INPUT 20   Telling a story or presenting facts in an interesting or dramatic way

You'll never believe this/it ... / You won't/may not believe this/it, but ...

This is hard to believe, but ...

Believe it or not ...

Can you imagine? (may also come *after* the 'interesting' fact)

And just imagine ... / Imagine my surprise when ...

And the surprising thing is ...

I was surprised to find out ...

Surprisingly/Strangely enough ...

I couldn't believe my eyes/ears! (may come *after* the interesting fact)

Do you know what happened then/to us/to me/yesterday/? etc.

(And then) (do) you know what he did/said?

What do you think he did?

And you know what?

Guess what! / You'll never guess (what happened next)!

Are you sitting down? / You'd better sit down!

And then, to add insult to injury ...

As if that wasn't enough, then ...

To cap it all ...

Sample dialogue

Original

Pat:	I've had an awful morning!
Doreen:	Oh dear. Come and have a cup of tea and tell me all about it.
Pat:	Well, I went to the cleaner's to pick up my dress and they said it won't be ready until tomorrow! Then when I got back to the car, a traffic warden was putting a ticket on it. £25!
Doreen:	Oh no! Poor you!

New version

Pat:	You'll never believe what an awful morning I've had!
Doreen:	Oh, really ...
Pat:	First I went to the cleaner's to pick up my dress, and guess what? It won't be ready till tomorrow! And you know what happened then? When I got back to the car I couldn't believe my eyes. A traffic warden was putting a ticket on it! £25! Can you imagine?
Doreen:	I see ...

4.   Students perform the new versions. Which Speaker A sounds most interesting? Students could vote.

5.   Change of roles: now the uninterested listener becomes the excited story-teller.

Follow-up options

1.   Introduce some phrases to react to surprising or shocking news (see INPUT 26). Ask students to perform the dialogue again, this time with the second character showing almost exaggerated interest and surprise.

2.   Get the students into pairs; one of them should start telling the story of a film, using as many of the new expressions as he/she can. The other should follow the story open mouthed, reacting regularly. If your students like absurd scenes, you may tell them to deliberately choose an extremely boring film to talk about.

Variation 1   Yes, but listen to this!

What happens when two extroverts meet? Since each person wants to sound more interesting than the other, they might try to outdo each other and therefore will use many of the expressions and narrative techniques above. They will also want to hold the floor as long as they can, adding more and more surprising or shocking facts, and for this, they can use further expressions like the ones listed in INPUT 21. Introduce these phrases and ask students to transform the dialogue into a conversation between two competing extroverts!

INPUT 21   Adding surprising or shocking elements to a story

And that's not all (of it)!
And there's more!
But wait, there's more!
And there's something else too!
And that's not the end of it!
And listen to this!

Link

Consider trying **I couldn't get a word in edgeways (8)** from the Conversational rules and structure section, and **Reactions (25)** from the Functions and meanings in conversation section as a follow-up to this activity.

Teacher's diary

Did students recognise the communicative potential of these narrative techniques? Did they succeed in using the phrases naturally? Do you think that doing the activity once is sufficient to teach these techniques? If not, how could you develop the activity to offer further practice?

SECTION III

FUNCTIONS AND MEANINGS IN CONVERSATION

Introduction

The first two sections of this book focus on how to prepare students to be smooth and efficient conversationalists through knowledge of, and practice in, certain standard conventions and strategies. So far, however, there has been no mention of what people actually say, that it, of the purpose and possible topics of conversation, or, in more general terms, of what meaning the speakers want to get across to their partners. This section will focus on such issues and the following summary includes indications of the activities which tackle each particular question.

Language functions

Since the communicative approach to language teaching appeared in the mid-1970s, language functions, e.g., agreeing, asking for information, making suggestions, etc., have played an important role in the language classroom. A typical feature of language functions is that they involve a great number of set phrases and structures, and these are usually taught thoroughly in contemporary coursebooks.

Apart from a general activity which can be used with all functions (**21 More of the same**), we have covered specifically only those language functions which are typical of conversational talk: asking and answering questions (**22 Questions and answers**), expressing and agreeing with opinion (**23 Oh yes, I agree**), disagreeing politely (**24 How to disagree politely**), and reacting in various ways to what a conversation partner is saying, e.g., expressing concern, sympathy, surprise, disbelief, etc., which helps keep the conversation going (**25 Reactions**).

Speech acts

Speech acts are utterances which, rather than just conveying information, actually carry out an action or language function. For example, the question, *'Would you open the window, please?'* is a way of getting the listener to open the window and therefore is an action. Similarly, *'I pronounce you man and wife'* or *'You're under arrest'* are also equivalent to actions.

Some speech acts are direct and straightforward, e.g., *'Put that gun down!'*, but the majority in everyday conversation are indirect. For example, the sentence, 'I wonder if you could post this letter for me' does not mean 'I'm curious whether you are able to post this letter', but is an indirect way of making the listener post the letter. Utterances like these are usually termed *indirect speech acts*.

Language learners, especially at an early stage, can easily misunderstand indirect speech acts and take what has been said at its face value. For example, when a group of Hungarian teenagers on an exchange programme recently in Britain were told by the English group leader, *'You want to be back here by five o'clock'* (= 'Be back by five o'clock!), someone answered, *'No, we don't. Can we come back at six?'*. Making learners aware that such structures have a 'surface' and a 'real' meaning can therefore be very important (**27 What they say and what they mean**).

Same meaning—different meaning

It is not only with indirect speech acts that the literal meaning of a language form differs from the deeper meaning; utterances often have subconscious, semiconscious or quite intentional undertones, and it is well worthwhile for students to spend some time getting to grips with and analysing these (**28 Paranoia or a hidden meaning in everything**). On the other hand, they should also be made aware that in some cases different language forms can have very similar meanings (**26 Change without changing**).

The cooperative principle

In the 1970s, the philosopher Paul Grice put forward a set of four general rules (he called them 'maxims') to describe how participants 'cooperate' in conversation to achieve smooth and efficient interaction:

1. **The maxim of quality**   do not say things which you believe to be untrue or for which you lack adequate evidence.
2. **The maxim of quantity**   say neither too little nor too much.
3. **The maxim of relevance**   what you say should be clearly relevant.
4. **The maxim of manner**   speak clearly; avoid obscurity and ambiguity.

The maxims thus claim that in efficient conversation it is assumed that the participants will not lie or bluff, will not be too brief not over-talkative, will not say completely irrelevant things and will try to be as clear as possible.

However, people are not perfect and sometimes they break these rules by accident, through misunderstanding or clumsiness, which can result in the conversation going astray. There are also occasions when people deliberately violate these principles for some reason, usually to express some subtle meaning. For example, we may say things which are obviously untrue to express irony or sarcasm, e.g., *'Of course, this government is just perfect! Look at our thriving economy!'*; we may be too brief, because we want to show that we are angry or want to discourage someone from talking, e.g., *'What's that you're reading?', 'A book.'*; we can be irrelevant to indicate reluctance to pursue the topic, e.g., *'Have you washed the car?' 'Oh, that blouse looks nice on you!'*; and we may consciously be obscure to hide some fact (just think of the way politicians speak).

Such indirect messages are delicate and may be difficult for language learners to understand, especially if they come from a culture which is very different from the target language culture; it can be useful therefore to draw their attention to this issue (**29 When you break the rules ...**).

21   More of the same

Level   Intermediate and advanced

Purpose   Focus on the new language function presented in the
                   dialogue

Dialogue type Any dialogue from a functional coursebook, i.e., with the
                   text centred around a particular language function

In this activity

Students become 'textbook writers' and rewrite the original dialogue in such a way
that the functional teaching purpose becomes more featured.

Preparation

1. Look through the dialogue you are going to use with your students and make a
   list of the phrases containing the highlighted language function in the text.

2. Collect three or four further phrases which carry out the same function and put
   them on the board/OHP.

In class

1. Tell the students that in this activity they will be working as textbook writers.

2. Introduce the dialogue and ask them to examine it from the teaching point of view:
   What is the dialogue trying to teach? (Obviously the particular language function.)
   How many different structures are introduced to carry out that function? Altogether
   how many times does the language function appear in the dialogue?

3. Tell them that the publishers are not satisfied with the dialogue because they believe
   that it could be made more useful. In fact, they would like to offer a contract
   to the team which can produce the best rewritten version, i.e., with the most
   functional expressions both in terms of types and total number.

4. Get the students to form teams of co-authors (groups of two or three) and ask
   them to prepare their proposals; these should contain (a) the authors' names, (b)
   the suggested title of the book, and (c) the rewritten dialogue. While writing,

students can refer to the list of expressions you have put on the board for further ideas.

5. When students have finished, ask the teams to read out their proposals in turn. Write the authors' names and the book title on the board, and during each reading record the number of expression types and the total number of expressions used.

6. Now the students turn into an editorial board and, by secret vote, decide on the version to be published.

Follow-up option

At home the students find and write out sentences from different texts which contain examples of the language function in question. The texts may vary from other units in the coursebook to pop songs, or from English radio and television programmes, films and videos to contemporary novels.

Variation 1   Titles

Present the original dialogue to the students and point out that it lacks a title. Students form co-author teams as in the activity above and invent a suitable title for the dialogue, which has something to do with what it teaches. Listen to the various titles, then tell students that according to the editor, the dialogue is not characteristic enough; the teams should rewrite it so that the text better suits the title they have given it.

Link

Consider trying **Change without changing (26)** and **What they say and what they mean (27)** from this section as a follow-up to this activity.

Teacher's diary

How did the students do in this activity? Did they use English when working together in the small groups? What other tasks do you know which teach language functions in a game-like fashion?

22   Questions and answers

Level   Elementary and above

Purpose   Practise asking for information and saying you do not know

Dialogue type   Any dialogue in which questions are asked

In this activity

Students extend the dialogue by making one speaker ask questions to which the other speaker does not know the answer.

Preparation

Look at the question and answer structures in INPUT 22 and select six to eight structures from both; make sure that you include a mixture of both formal and informal versions.

In class

1. Tell students that you are a receptionist/secretary/porter/clerk — you could even put on a peaked cap or reading glasses! — and they have to ask you for some information (which you specify) in as many different ways as they can think of. Put the structures they mention on the board/OHP, and then elicit some more informal structures which, for example, friends or family could use with each other. Add the structures they have not mentioned from your own list.

2. Meanwhile, you have been answering their requests by saying you do not know in different ways (see INPUT 22). Ask students now if they remember your answers and put these too on the board/OHP.

3. Students get into pairs or small groups, depending on the number of characters in the dialogue. Their task is to prepare a variation of the dialogue in which they add three different questions of the type discussed. These questions should ideally be very difficult so that the person who is being asked does not know the answers and is therefore a bit embarrassed and apologetic.

4. The pairs or groups perform the new version of the dialogue. It's up to them how the dialogue ends — the person who asks the questions might get very frustrated!

INPUT 22   Asking for information and answering that you do not know

Asking for information

(Excuse me) do you know . . . ?
Would/Do you happen to know . . . ?
Can/Could you tell me . . . , please?
I wonder if you could tell me . . . ?
I was wondering (if you could help me) . . .
Would you mind telling me . . . ?
Sorry to trouble/bother you, but (do you know) . . . ?
Can/Could you give me any information about/on . . . , please?
(I hope you don't mind my asking, but) I'd like to know/enquire about . . .
I'm interested in . . .
Could I ask . . . ? / I'd like to ask . . .
Could you find out . . . please?
When/Where/What/etc. do you think it/he will . . . ?
Have you (got) any idea about . . . ?
And you've no idea when/where/etc. . . . ?
Know anything about . . . ?

Answering you do not know

(I'm afraid) I don't know (yet).
I'm (terribly) sorry I (really) don't know.
I've no idea, I'm afraid.
I'm sorry I can't help you there.
I'm afraid I couldn't say.
I have to say/admit I don't know a great deal about . . .
I can't answer that one (but I'll tell you where you can find out).
I can't decide/make up my mind.
I'm not (too/really) sure.
I couldn't tell you off-hand, I'm afraid.
I forget / I don't/can't remember.
It's slipped my mind.
I wish I knew.
Don't ask me.
I haven't got a clue.
I'll have to think about it / think it over.

Follow-up options

1. One of Columbo, the television detective's favourite ways of getting information is by casually asking everyday questions. Students rewrite the dialogue by turning the speaker who asks questions into Columbo at work. The person being asked should at first politely, and then speaking much more directly, pretend he/she does not know the answer.

2. Some people love asking lots of questions, which can often irritate the poor receptionist/shopkeeper or whoever happens to be on the receiving end. Students prepare a new version of the dialogue by making Speaker A ask far too many questions so that Speaker B slowly loses patience!

Variation 1 Enquiring over the phone

Calling an office or institute to make enquiries is something that most language learners will sooner or later have to do. In such cases people often use question forms that are typical of telephone conversations (see INPUT 23). Introduce some structures of this sort and then ask students to turn the original dialogue into a telephone conversation and add further questions to it.

INPUT 23 Enquiring over the phone

	calling		ask about ...
I'm	phoning	to	enquire ...
	ringing		find out ...

I'm calling about ...
I'd like to ask/enquire about/know if ...
Can/Could you give any information about/on ... please?
I'd appreciate it if you could give me some information on ...
I wonder if you could tell me (about) ... ?
I was wondering if you could help me. I'd like to know ...
Can/Could you tell me ... ?
I'd like to talk to someone who has information about/on ...
Sorry to trouble you, but is ... ?
And you've no idea when/what/where/etc. ... ?

---

3. If the original dialogue is between an official, waiter, shopkeeper, etc. and a member of the public, a nice twist to it can be to imagine that the usual official, etc. has had to leave for a few minutes and has asked a friend to stand in for him/her. This friend, of course, does not know any of the answers to the questions he/she is asked.

Link

Consider trying **I'm afraid I can't (9)** from the Conversational rules and structure section, and Variation 2 of **Buying time: fillers (11)** from the Conversational strategies section as a follow-up to this activity.

Teacher's diary

Did students realise that some phrases and structures were more formal and polite than others? Did they use them appropriately?

---

23 Oh yes, I agree

Level   Elementary and above

Purpose   Provide ways of expressing and agreeing with an opinion

Dialogue type   Any dialogue

In this activity

Students extend the original dialogue. One speaker keeps expressing opinions on related topics and the other speaker politely agrees with these.

Preparation

1. Collect a number of phrases and structures that are used (a) to express an opinion and (b) to agree with an opinion. Put them on the board/OHP (see INPUT 24).

> NOTE: *One of the most common features of everyday conversation is that it contains many expressions of opinion followed promptly by an agreement from the other speaker (often only out of politeness). In this way conversation can proceed smoothly.*

2. (For **Follow-up option 1**:) Prepare enough cue cards so that there is one for every student, each containing one phrase or structure to express agreement.

In class

1. Start the class by asking the students to express opinions that they think everyone will agree with, and see how many different ways of agreeing the others can come up with. Introduce the list of phrases and structures you have collected and briefly discuss with the students why they are useful in conversation.

2. Students get into pairs or small groups, depending on the number of speakers in the dialogue. Ask them to extend the dialogue by adding extra sentences to express opinions on related topics, with which the other speaker then agrees (see **Sample dialogue** below). At least two expressions of opinion for each speaker should be added.

3. Students perform their versions.

INPUT 24   Expressing opinion and agreement with an opinion

Expressing opinion

I (personally) think/believe/feel . . .
Personally, I believe/think/feel . . .
I honestly feel . . .
In my (personal) opinion/view . . .
I imagine/suppose/reckon . . .
Do you know what I think? I
  think . . .
As I see it . . .
The way I look at it/see it . . .
It appears/seems to me . . .
To my mind . . .
If you ask me . . .
I'd say that . . .
As far as I can tell . . .
Let me tell you . . .
To the best of my knowledge . . .
I'm pretty/quite sure that . . .
I'm fairly certain that . . .
It's quite obvious that . . .

Expressing agreement with an opinion

Yes/yeah
(Yes) it is, isn't it? / He does,
  doesn't he? / etc.
Exactly/quite/absolutely/definitely.
Right / All right / You're quite right.
That's (quite) right/true.
How true / True/fair enough.
Quite so.
Of course.
Yes/well I suppose so.
I agree (entirely) / I think so, too.
I couldn't agree more.
That's just/exactly what I think/
  thought/was thinking.
That's what I was going to say.
You took the words out of my
  mouth!
That's a good point.
So/neither do I / Me too.

Follow-up options

1. Give one of the cue cards you have prepared to every student. They are going to perform the dialogue again, but this time they must include the phrase or structure on their card at least twice. Students watching the performances try to work out every participant's phrase. They can make the audience's job more difficult by introducing other phrases as well, but these phrases must not be used more than once.

2. This time ask students to overdo the opinion-adding and agreement parts so that the speakers spend most of their time reflecting on each others' remarks rather than getting on with the dialogue.

Sample dialogue

Original

Anne: One gin and tonic and . . . what will you have, Sandra?
Sandra: A glass of sparkling mineral water, please.
Barman: Right you are, ladies. Anything else?
Sandra: Yes, two packets of peanuts, please.
Barman: There you go.

New version

Anne: One gin and tonic and . . . what will you have, Sandra?
Sandra: A glass of sparkling mineral water please. I think it's more refreshing than alcohol.
Barman: Quite right, madam. Very refreshing on a hot day like this.
Anne: If you ask me, a stiff gin and tonic does you more good when you're tired.
Sandra: Well yes, I suppose so. In my opinion, you should just drink what you feel like when you feel like it.
Anne: I couldn't agree more. Let's have some peanuts, too.

Variation 1   Yes sir, I agree entirely, sir

Students change the characters in the dialogue into good old clichés: the slightly stupid boss who has a firm opinion about everything, and the servile employee who is all too ready to agree to whatever his/her boss says. The sillier the things the boss says and the more wholeheartedly the employee agrees, the funnier the situation could become.

Link

Consider trying Variation 1 in **Relax and chat (1)** from the Conversational rules and structure section, **How to disagree politely (24)** from this section and **Let's not be so polite! (32)** from the Social and cultural contexts section as a follow-up to this activity.

Teacher's diary

Did students succeed in making the agreements sound natural or did they tend to turn the speakers in the dialogue into 'caricatures' (as in the Variation)? Did they find it difficult to use the proper intonation? How much agreement occurs in conversation in their own culture?

24 How to disagree politely

Level   Intermediate and advanced

Purpose   Develop ability to overcome politely the difficulty of disagreeing with someone

Dialogue type   Dialogue containing opinions, explanations, arguments, etc., which could be disagree with

In this activity

Students make one of the characters disagree politely with what the other is saying.

Preparation

1. Go through the dialogue and mark the places where one speaker could disagree with the other. Note that the places you mark might not always be at the end of a speaker's turn.

2. List some polite ways of disagreeing (see INPUT 25 for some ideas).

In class

1. Ask students to imagine they are talking to someone like an elderly neighbour or relative, their head teacher or boss, their driving instructor, or a stranger who is older than them, and they disagree strongly with what this person is saying. Do they just nod and smile to avoid an unpleasant moment? (You might demonstrate this.) Or do they dare to disagree? If so, what might they say?

2. Tell students you are, for example, the head teacher and say something controversial, e.g. *'People under sixteen shouldn't be allowed out after nine o'clock.'* The class brainstorms polite ways of disagreeing; put their ideas along with those you collected on the board/OHP.

3. Go through the dialogue with the students and show them the disagreement points you marked in preparation.

4. In pairs, students make one character politely disagree several times with the other. It is up to each pair how the second character reacts to this, and whether the dialogue ends peacefully or angrily.

INPUT 25 Polite ways of disagreeing

I agree with you, but ... / Agreed/Granted, but ...
I couldn't agree more, but ...
Yes/Yeah/Sure, but (on the other hand) ...
You're right, but ...
That's a good idea, but / Yes, that's quite true, but ...

I see what you mean, but ... / I see/take your point, but ...
Well, you have a point there, but ...
I can see why you think/say that, but ...
That's one way of looking at it, but ...
There's a lot of truth in what you say, but/still/however ...

Yes, maybe/perhaps/possibly, but ... / That may be so, but ...
I would agree, only/but ... / I agree in principle, but ...
Perhaps/Yes, but don't you think ... ?
In most cases you would be right, but ...
To a certain extent yes, but ... / Yes, up to a point, but ...
That would be great, except ...

(Yes, but) I think it's not so much (a case of) ...
I think perhaps it's more a case of ...
But isn't it more a matter/question of ... ? / more to do with ... ?
Yes, but don't forget ... / but we shouldn't forget ...
Perhaps not quite as bad/good/difficult as that ...
But surely ...
Er ... I don't know ...

Forgive me if I'm wrong, but ...
Sorry, I don't quite see it the same way ...
I'm not sure (I quite agree with that part about) ...
I don't think it's quite that simple; you see ...
Actually/In fact, I think ... (followed by a different opinion)
Personally, I'm more inclined to agree with ... (someone else)
Personally, I wouldn't go so far as (to say) that ...

---

5. Each pair performs their version for the others, who might want to note down
    how many different ways of disagreeing they hear.

Follow-up options

1. Introduce some more disagreement phrases and put these on the board/OHP as
    well. Students take a vote on (a) which ones they personally like most, and (b)

which they think would be most useful when trying to convince a police officer or traffic warden not to fine them. Everybody has three votes for both categories. The votes are added up on the board, with the students dictating them one after the other and a 'secretary' putting tally marks in front of the expressions voted for. This way, without realising it, students go through the whole list several times!

2. In pairs or groups, students choose four or five phrases from the list and arrange them in order of politeness, starting with the most polite. They might add a couple of rude ones, e.g., *'You're wrong'*, or *'Rubbish!'* to the bottom of their list. When they perform the dialogue, the character who disagrees can use these in order, getting less and less polite as he/she gets more and more impatient.

Variation 1   Difficult to disagree

In groups of three, students act out a variation of the original dialogue in which Speaker A disagrees politely with Speaker B, but this time they add a Speaker C who supports and agrees all the time with Speaker B (see INPUT 24 for agreement phrases); this makes Speaker A's job even harder!

Link

Consider trying **I'm afraid I can't (9)** from the Conversational rules and structure section, **Oh yes, I agree (23)** from this section, and **Let's not be so polite! (32)** from the Social and cultural contexts section as a follow-up to this activity.

Teacher's diary

Is disagreeing in the students' own culture more or less acceptable than in English? Is there anyone you must not disagree with? Do the students' first languages contain as many phrases of disagreement as English does?

---

25   Reactions

Level   Elementary and above

Purpose   Provide a repertoire of phrases to react to what people say

Dialogue type Any dialogue in which someone tells a story or where the speeches are longer

In this activity

Students add unexpected sentences to one speaker's part which require various reactions from the other speaker.

Preparation

1. Have a look at the list of reactions in INPUT 26 and select a few from each category that you would like to teach your students.

INPUT 26   Reacting to what the other speaker says

I'm listening/following

Yes/Uh-huh/mh-hmm.
I see/know (what you mean).
Quite (so).
Right/okay/exactly/sure.
(How) interesting!
Really?
Is that right?
Me too / So do I / Neither would I / etc.
And so? / And what happened (then)? / Yes? / And (then)? / Does he? / Did it? / Are they? / Has it? / (and any short questions)

I'm surprised!

Really?
No!/Never!
It can't be!
Gosh!/Wow!/Phew!/Oh!?
Impossible!
What?! / Where?! / Who?! / etc.
I don't/can't believe you/it!
What a surprise! / That *is* a surprise!
(That's) incredible/amazing!
Can you believe it?!
He didn't! / They haven't! / You're not! / He doesn't! / etc.
A gun?! / In the bathroom?! / Did she?! / Are they?! / Tomorrow?! / Only?! / (any similar echo question)

93

INPUT 26 (*continued*)

Have they really? / Did he really? / etc.
You can't be serious! / Are you serious?
You are/must be kidding/joking!
My goodness!
Bloody hell! (and other swear words)

I sympathise

Oh dear!
Oh no!
Oh, what/that's a pity/shame!
Oh, my God!
How/That's unfortunate!
You must be very annoyed/upset!
That's too bad!
It must have been awful/horrible/terrible!
Oh, how / That's awful/horrible/terrible!
I know (exactly) how you feel / how it feels / what you mean!
I know the feeling!
Oh, I'm sorry about/to hear that.
I'm really/terribly/extremely/very sorry!
I'm ever so sorry!
I do sympathise!
You poor thing! / Poor you!

I'm pleased to hear that

Oh good!
I'm (ever) so glad!
Well done!
Good for you!
(Hey) (that's) great/fantastic/ wonderful/brilliant!
That is (really) good news!
I'm very/really pleased (to hear that).
Well, isn't that great/wonderful/ etc.!

I find it difficult to believe

Oh, come on!
Are you sure?
Really?
Oh?
What!
It can't be!
Surely not!
Is that right?
I don't/can't believe it!
You're kidding/joking, aren't you?
Are you pulling my leg?

2.   Prepare cue cards with two different reactions on each. For example:

> | |
> |---|
> | Oh no! |
> | Good for you! |

> | |
> |---|
> | I can't believe it! |
> | Well done! |

In class

1.   Ask students to think of sentences to say which contain good or bad news or something surprising or shocking, e.g., *'I've just won £20 000!'* or *'There won't be any school tomorrow'*. Students say these sentences and each time you give an appropriate short reaction.

2.   Discuss the fact that conversation in English is full of reactions like this because they show that (a) you are listening and interested in what your partner is saying, (b) you would like to encourage them to continue the conversation. Show students the different categories of reactions you have collected and practise saying them individually and with different combinations of students. Intonation is important here, remember!

3.   Students get into pairs or groups. Give a cue card to one student in each pair or group, telling them not to show it to their partner(s). This student must add (or change) two sentences to (in) his/her part in the dialogue to elicit from the other(s) reactions like the ones on the card (see **Sample dialogue**).

4.   The pairs or groups perform the dialogue with the improvised parts, and these watching work out what kind of reactions were written on the cue cards.

Sample dialogue

Original

A: ... so she gave me their telephone number and asked me to call back next week.

B: Will there be a new delivery before then?

A: I hope so.

Student A's cue card:

> | |
> |---|
> | 1. Hey, that's great! |
> | 2. Where?!! |

Sample dialogue (*continued*)

New version

A: . . . so she gave me their telephone number and said that if I call back next week, they'll definitely have some then!

B: Hey, that's great! (or: That's really good news!, etc.) So there will be a delivery before then?

A: Yes, they've ordered some from Istanbul.

B: Where??!

Follow-up options

1. Students give a further performance of the extended dialogues, only this time ask them to really exaggerate the reactions. You may demonstrate how to do this beforehand: students call out reactions from the list and you repeat them with exaggerated intonation and facial expressions.

2. Textbook dialogues usually lack short reactions to signal 'I'm listening/following', especially noises like '*uhuh*' and '*mm-hmm*', and single words like 'Yes', 'No', 'Sure', 'Right', etc., which are a very important part of conversation. Ask students to perform the dialogue again, this time frequently inserting short reactions like these, accompanied by nodding.

3. Students get into different pairs. Student A has a cue card with a reaction on it and tries to elicit exactly that reaction (word for word) from Student B by saying sentences one after the other. If they do not succeed first time, they must keep trying! For example:

It can't be!	A: *The exam is tomorrow!* B: *Oh no!* A: *I mean, it's tomorrow, not Friday!* B: *Really?! How awful!* A: *Yes, and I think it's the biology exam!* B: *It can't be!*

Variation 1   Wrong reactions

Students perform the dialogue inserting the extra bits and the subsequent reactions (as in the activity above), but this time they should turn the performance into a comedy by providing wrong reactions. For example, if one speaker says, '*And just imagine, he lost his luggage at the airport!*', the other speaker could say, '*That's great! I'm ever so glad!*'. After this the dialogue could carry on in two ways:

The first speaker goes on as if nothing unusual had happened.
He/she could stop, look shocked and say something like, *'What do you mean?! It's really awful. He has no clothes and his keys are in his suitcase'*, to which an apology and a proper reaction is due.

Alternatively, students could give the right reactions but with the wrong intonation and facial expression, e.g., a sympathy reaction with a big happy smile.

Link

Consider trying Variation 1 in **Relax and chat (1)** from the Conversational rules and structure section, and **You'll never believe this! (20)** and **Oh yes, I agree (23)** from this section as a follow-up to this activity.

Teacher's diary

Many language learners find showing surprise, sympathy, etc. in English difficult and embarrassing; was this true of your students? If so, was the intonation the most difficult thing? Are such reactions common and important in their own language?

26   Change without changing

Level	Intermediate and advanced
Purpose	Develop linguistic creativity; demonstrate that any given conversation could have several equal variations
Dialogue type	Any dialogue

In this activity

Students make alterations to every sentence of the dialogue, leaving the meaning intact.

Preparation

1. Take a short exchange from a dialogue the students know and prepare a new version of it in which you change every sentence (using synonym words and structures) *without* changing the meaning of the sentences (see **Sample dialogue**).

Sample dialogue

Original

Paul: Why are you standing up there, Mum?
Mum: There's a mouse! I saw a mouse! I hate mice!
Paul: Don't worry, Mum. I'll get rid of it. Where is it now?

New version

Paul: What are you doing up on that chair, Mum?
Mum: A mouse! I've just seen a mouse! I can't stand mice!
Paul: There's no need to panic, Mum. I'll chase it out. Which way did it go?

---

2. Write the two versions on the board/OHP.

In class

1. Just because we choose to say something in a certain way does not mean that there are no other ways to do so; different forms can have very similar meaning. Present the exchanges you have prepared to demonstrate this.

98

2. Students get into pairs or groups and make similar changes to every sentence of the dialogue. A sentence can be considered changed if at least two words have been replaced or removed.

3. Students prepare the variations, then read them out. How similar to or different from each other are the new versions?

Follow-up options

1. With the whole class together, pick out some important sentences from the dialogue, i.e., ones which contain some new material, and get the students to say as many variations as they can. This can also be a competition: Students in small groups write down as many variations they can think of in, say, five minutes.

2. A fluency exercise: Students work in small groups and only one person has the text of the dialogue in front of him/her. He/she reads out the dialogue sentence by sentence, and after each sentence one student must produce an immediate variation. Students should take turns and the aim is to go through the dialogue as quickly as possible.

3. For homework, students have to rewrite the dialogue, changing every sentence.

Variation 1   Interpreting from English into English

Students get into groups so that in each group there is someone for every role plus one interpreter. They should act out the dialogue (without looking at the text) with the interpreter 'translating', that is, reformulating each sentence from English into different English! The participants should take the situation very seriously and wait for the 'translation' before making any response. It can be fun if the interpreter interprets what he/she hears in a much lengthier or much shorter way.

Link

Consider trying **Dialogue halves (5)** from the Conversational rules and structure section, **In other words (16)** from the Conversational strategies section, and **Formal−informal (33)** from the Social and cultural contexts section as a follow-up to this activity.

Teacher's diary

Did students get better or quicker at thinking of variations with practice? What kind of changes did they find most difficult to make? Do you agree that language creativity can be developed through doing such exercises?

---

27 What they say and what they mean

Level   Intermediate and advanced

Purpose   Explore the relationship between the surface and real
                   meanings of indirect requests, suggestions and advice

Dialogue type Dialogue containing suggestions, advice and/or requests

In this activity

Students rewrite the dialogue so that the speakers take every utterance at its face value
and ignore (or deliberately misunderstand) the real meaning of the phrases.

Preparation

1. Go through the dialogue and underline all the phrases or sentences where the speaker
    wants the hearer to do something. Typical examples are commands, requests,
    suggestions, advice, etc. (see INPUT 27).

2. Choose one such phrase from the dialogue whose meaning when taken literally
    is different from what the speaker actually means by saying it. For example, *'Why
    don't we go there?'* is not really a question but a suggestion; if it were understood
    as a question, the person addressed might answer, *'Because we don't want to!'*

In class

1. Write the example you have chosen on the board and discuss with the students
    the difference between what it would mean literally and what it really means when
    used in conversation.

2. Explain to the students that in conversation people often use phrases like *'Can
    you . . . ?'*, *'Why don't we . . . ?'* and *'If I were you . . . '* when making requests,
    suggestions or giving advice. Because these are indirect, they can sometimes
    confuse language learners.

INPUT 27 Common phrases to request, suggest and advise

Requests for action

Please . . . (. . . , will/would you?)

Will/Would/Could/Can you please . . .

. . . , will/would you please?

Would/Do you mind . . . (please)?

Do you think you could . . . (please)?

Do you think it would be possible (for you) to . . . ?

Would it be possible for you to . . . ?

Would there be any possibility of . . . ?

Would you be so kind as to . . . ?

Would you be kind enough to . . . ?

Can/Could you . . . for me, please?

Could you possibly . . . ?

I'd appreciate it if you could . . .

I'd be (very/most) grateful if you could . . .

Can/Could I ask you to . . . ?

I must/have to ask you to . . . (I'm afraid)

I'd like you to . . . (please)

You couldn't . . . could you?

You (may) want to . . .

You'd better . . .

Suggestions/advice

What/How about . . . ?

Why don't we/you . . . ?

Why not . . . ?

I suggest . . . ing / I suggest you/we . . .

I'd like to suggest / May I suggest . . .

If I may/might make a suggestion . . .

Shall we . . . ?

Let's . . . (. . . , shall we?)

Couldn't you/we . . . ?

We/You could/might (try) . . .

We/You can/could always . . .

Perhaps/Surely we/you could . . . ?

(If I were you) I would . . .

We might as well . . .

I('ll) tell you what: we'll . . .

You may/might want/like to . . .

Have you ever considered/ thought of . . . ?

I was wondering if you'd ever thought of . . .

(I think) you should/ought to/ you'd better . . .

The best thing would be to . . .

It would be best if . . .

One way would be to . . .

(Don't/do you think) it might be an idea to . . . ?

Would/Might it be an idea to . . .

3. Go through all the phrases of indirect requests, suggestions, etc. in the dialogue and ask students to think of synonym structures for each of them (you may also suggest some — see INPUT 27).
4. Students get into pairs or groups and rewrite the dialogue by deliberately misunderstanding the direct requests or suggestions, that is, taking them at their face value. This is likely to change the complete course of the dialogue (see **Sample dialogue**).

Sample dialogue

Original

A: While you're there tomorrow, can you please tell Peter about Thursday's meeting?
B: Yes, sure. But if I were you, I'd phone him now.
A: Oh, OK. He might be there. I'll try.

New version

A: While you're there tomorrow, can you please tell Peter about Thursday's meeting?
B: Yes I can, but I don't want to.
A: Do it, please.
B: OK. But if I were you, I'd phone him now.
A: You're not me ... etc.

Follow-up options

1. Elicit from the students as many ways of suggesting and requesting as they can think of; put the phrases on the board and add some new ones as well (see INPUT 27). Students go through the original dialogue again, and decide which of the phrases on the board could substitute those in the dialogue. Check their lists and discuss with them why some phrases would not be appropriate in certain contexts.

2. In pairs or small groups, students perform the dialogue, inserting additional suggestions or requests. You can personalise this activity by asking everybody to choose their favourite phrase, which they then have to include in their parts twice. The audience must spot everyone's favourite phrase or structure.

Variation 1   The hinting game

Students replace the suggestions, requests, orders, etc. in the original dialogue with much more indirect ways of suggesting, requesting, ordering etc., that is, speakers make statements which only give hints as to what they want the other to do. For example, the Sample dialogue above might read:

A: *You'll be there tomorrow, won't you? You know, Peter works there. He might want to know about Thursday's meeting ...*

B: *All right, I'll tell him if I can find him. It might be easier to phone him, though. He's probably there now, actually.*

A: *Well, I suppose I can try and phone him.*

Link

Consider trying **Paranoia or a hidden meaning in everything (28)** from this section, and **Let's not be so polite (32)** from the Social and cultural contexts section as a follow-up to this activity.

Teacher's diary

Which of the phrases in INPUT 27, if any, were students most reluctant to use? Did students recognise the relationship between politeness and different ways of making requests, suggestions? Did students tend to use the more direct ways of making requests or suggestions rather than the indirect ones?

---

28 Paranoia or a hidden meaning in everything

Level Intermediate and advanced

Purpose Explore the relationship between the surface meaning of utterances and the possible hidden underlying message

Dialogue type Any dialogue

In this activity

Students perform the dialogue in such a way that each sentence is followed by an 'echo' which is an underlying hidden meaning of the sentence.

Preparation

Write a short sample dialogue and one or two 'echo' sentences after each sentence, in which a possible hidden meaning is brought to the surface. The Sample dialogue below may give you ideas.

In class

1. Read out your sample dialogue without the echoes, then go through it sentence by sentence and discuss with the students what possible hidden meanings they can think of. Show them the echoes you have collected.

2. Students get into small groups so that there are two people in each group for every role in the dialogue they are going to use. One will read out his/her original lines and the other will provide the 'echo' of those lines.

3. In these small groups, students invent the 'echo' parts. Encourage them not to be afraid of silly interpretations.

4. The dialogues are performed with the echoes echoing.

Sample dialogue

J: That's a nice jacket, Dick. Very flattering.

(*Echo*:   It hides your beer belly. Or: I bet it was expensive.)

D: Thank you, John. Nice of you to say so.

(*Echo*:   You don't usually say nice things. What do you want? Or: I
             hate it when you make trivial comments.)

J: Have you got all the documents with you?

(*Echo*:   You usually leave something important at home. Or: I always
             have to check up on you.)

D: Yes, yes. I'm ready to start the meeting now, if you'd like to
             call the others.

(*Echo*:   Go and do something useful. Or: Please remember that I'm you
             superior and not the other way round.)

Follow-up options

1.   Once students get the hang of interpreting the hidden meanings of texts, it can
     be quite funny to take some 'innocent' texts and create hidden messages underlying
     them. Students could use the introduction of their coursebook or some grammar
     explanation, etc., or perhaps speeches of wellknown politicians or educational
     authorities the students know, e.g., the head teacher.

2.   This time ask students, in pairs, to write a short and a very trivial dialogue. Then
     each pair should be joined by another; students in one pair read out their dialogue,
     while the two other people provide an immediate, spontaneous 'echo' interpreting
     the hidden meaning of the sentences. Afterwards the two pairs should change roles.

3.   One popular idea, much loved by film directors, is to have a man and a woman
     who are attracted to each other and are having what seems to be a trivial
     conversation, but both of them are reading hidden meanings into what the other
     is saying. Students could try this in groups of four, a man, a woman and two echoes.

Variation 1   Be over-sensitive

Students rewrite the dialogue in such a way that one speaker is over-sensitive, almost
paranoid, and detects a hidden meaning in everything the other person says; he/she
reacts to these hidden messages, e.g, *'So you mean . . .', 'So you are saying . . .'*,
etc. (see INPUT 17) and the other speaker must reassure him/her that there is no
hidden meaning before the dialogue can go on. For example:

S2: *You just relax. I'll make coffee this time.*
S2: *You mean you don't like the way I make coffee?*
S1: *No, of course I don't mean that. I just thought I'd save you the trouble.*
S2: *Are you trying to say I'm getting old? Is that it?*

Link

Consider trying Variation 1 in **In other words (16)** from the Conversational strategies section, and **What they say and what they mean (27)** and Variation 1 in **When you break the rules . . . (29)** from this section as a follow-up to this activity.

Teacher's diary

Consider the hidden meanings your students and you came up with. Were they all negative? Did students agree that hidden meanings have an important role in conversation? How well did they do in finding possible hidden meanings?

29 When you break the rules . . .

Level   Advanced

Purpose   Explore the effect on conversation of breaking important
conversational rules

Dialogue type Any dialogue

In this activity

Students rewrite the dialogue deliberately breaking one of the major conversational rules.

Four important conversational rules

1. **The truth rule**   — do not say things which you believe to be
untrue or for which you lack adequate
evidence
2. **The quantity rule**   — say neither too little nor too much
3. **The relevance rule** — what you say should be clearly relevant
4. **The clarity rule**   — speak clearly; avoid obscurity and
ambiguity

Preparation

1. Write the above conversational rules on the board/OHP.

2. Take a suitable short exchange from the dialogue which the students will be using
and prepare four versions of it, each one breaking one of the rules; write these,
too, on the board/OHP. Alternatively, you may want to use the sample dialogues
below.

NOTE: *Linguists refer to these four rules as Grice's conversational maxims; for a
more detailed summary, see the Introduction to this section.*

Sample dialogue

Normal answer
Abnormal answers

        A: *Where are you going?*
        B: *To buy some stamps.*

Breaking the **truth** rule: B: *To the Moon.*
Breaking the **quantity** rule: B: *To the door, then down the stairs, then out into the street, then ...*
Breaking the **relevance** rule: B: *Have you called your mother yet?*
Breaking the **clarity** rule: B: *I'm going to get something to put on a letter.*

In class

1. Introduce the four conversational rules and explain to the students that when people are having a conversation, they usually try to keep these rules and expect their conversation partner to do the same.

2. Point out that sometimes these rules are broken by accident, e.g., because of a misunderstanding, but at other times people break them deliberately. Present the sample dialogues you have prepared, and ask students first to decide which rule is broken in each case, and then to think about why someone might want to deliberately break these rules. Examples could be because they feel angry or irritated, because they are joking or being sarcastic, etc.

3. Get the students into small groups and ask them to rewrite the dialogue breaking

Sample dialogue

Original

A: Let's go to the cinema tonight. There's a brilliant film on.
B: Great idea. What's the film?
A: 'Cross Purposes' with Cheryl Strain and Tom Trip.
B: Sounds good.

New version (breaking the **relevance** rule)

A: Let's go to the cinema tonight. There's a brilliant film on.
B: When did you say you had to finish that essay by?
A: Oh, stop going on about that! I've got plenty of time to do it!
B: Not if you keep going out in the evening.

one of the four rules at the beginning of it and then changing the rest of the conversation accordingly (see **Sample dialogue** below).

4. The small groups perform their versions while the others listen and try to decide which rule was broken.

Follow-up options

1. Discuss with the students after each performance which rule was broken and how this affected the course of the dialogue. Was there usually some kind of argument or conflict in the conversation after breaking the rule?

2. Ask students to write a conversation for homework which is based, if possible, on a real experience from their family life in which a family member breaks one of the four rules.

3. Point out to students that being polite often involves breaking these rules. Ask them to look through some dialogues they know and find polite speech which does not strictly keep to one or more of the rules. Alternatively, go through the politeness strategies in INPUT 28 with them and discuss which of these are not compatible with the above rules.

Variation 1   How to be irritating

Usually in conversation people try to avoid conflicts. Breaking one of the above rules, however, often leads to a conflict if the person who breaks it is angry with the other speaker. Look again at the first sample dialogue and get the students to imagine how they would feel if they got answers like those. Then ask them to turn the dialogue into a conflict situation or quarrel, with both speakers breaking one or more of the rules.

Link

Consider trying **Going off the point (19)** from the Conversational strategies section, Variation 1 in **What they say and what they mean (27)** from this section, and **Let's not be so polite (32)** from the Social and cultural contexts section as a follow-up to this activity.

Teacher's diary

Did students find that some of the rules do not really apply to their own mother tongue? In the students' opinion, which rule is broken most often? Which is the most important?

SECTION IV

SOCIAL AND CULTURAL CONTEXTS

Introduction

Every conversation has a *time* and a *place* and a *social context* within a particular *culture*. The participants may not realise it but conversation is in many ways determined by these *external contextual factors*. For example, a particular conversation between a father and a daughter about money is likely to be completely different if it takes place in northern Alaska from if it takes place in southern Italy, at 3 p.m. from at 3 a.m., at the president's reception from in a pub, and between Americans from between Japanese. In fact, a lack of awareness of social and cultural language rules can be the source of much more difficulty to language learners than gaps in their grammar knowledge.

The fact that language is significantly determined by the context it is used in has been the topic of a great deal of research in linguistics, and the study of such issues comes under the terms *sociolinguistics* and *pragmatics*. In this section we have highlighted the following sociolinguistic/pragmatic issues with indications of the activities which focus on each one.

Time and location

The importance of time is recognised, for example, in Indian music, where different 'ragas' are composed for different times of the day; it is considered most inappropriate to play a morning raga in the evening. As for location, every place is believed to have its own atmosphere, which is attested to by the ever-growing industry of international tourism. Research has also confirmed that time and place are powerful factors, and their effect on conversation is worth pointing out to students (**31 Another time, another place . . .**).

The social situation

Some social events require different behaviour from some others. For example, a beach party is an entirely different social situation from a university degree ceremony, and as people are usually aware of such differences, they adjust their language accordingly. If they do not, they are likely to be on the receiving end of comments like *'He behaved as though he was at a football match'* or *'You're not at home now, you know'* (Variation 1 in **31 Social settings, 34 Family version**).

Office and status

A person's *office* is his/her job or profession, rank (military or other) and positions held, e.g., chairperson of the local council. *Status* refers to social standing or position in the social hierarchy and is determined by factors like age, education, family background, wealth. A person's office and status tend to determine how they talk and are talked to in conversation (**30 Who is the new one?**). When someone does not follow the expected patterns of conversational behaviour in this matter, they might elicit comments like *'I would never have thought she was a minister'* or *'He treated me like a VIP. What a laugh!'*.

The social norms of appropriate language use — style and politeness

The two most important (and interrelated) dimensions of linguistic appropriacy are how *formal* or *informal* the style is and what *degree of politeness* is present in the speech.

The *formal—informal continuum* is a measure of how much attention people pay to their speech. When they speak most naturally and casually, their style is informal, which is appropriate when both speakers are of more or less equal status. In contrast, the more carefully we attend to our speech production, the more formal it becomes, which is appropriate in formal contexts and between people of different office or status.

The *degree of politeness* does not depend entirely on the degree of formality (informal speech, for example, is not necessarily impolite!); it refers to the extent people want to make the other person feel comfortable in conversation, either because, for example, they respect the person and his/her privacy, or because they would like something from him/her. There are several typical politeness strategies, and language learners can benefit a lot from knowing and being able to use these (**32 Let's not be so polite!** and Variation 1 **Be more polite**).

Crosscultural differences

Conversation is heavily loaded with cultural information, which becomes apparent when members of very different cultures meet. Crosscultural differences affect conversation at every level and, in fact, very few of the rules and strategies described in this book are universal (this point often comes up in the Teacher's diaries). Language learners tend not to realise that a lack of crosscultural awareness and sensitivity can cause more serious misunderstandings, and indeed communication breakdowns, than an incorrectly used tense or wrong word order. There are so many culture-specific dos and don'ts that without any knowledge of these, a language learner is constantly walking through a cultural minefield (**35 How would it go at home? 36 Cultural differences and taboos**).

This brief overview demonstrates, we hope, the importance of sociocultural factors in conversation. Just imagine what difficulties a visitor from another planet might have in communicating with humans, even if he/she/it had a reasonable command of the vocabulary and grammar of a human language. In fact, that is exactly what students have to imagine in the last activity in the book (**37 Visitor from Mars**)!

30 Who is the new one?

Level Intermediate and above

Purpose Explore how status, office and personal style are reflected in conversation

Dialogue type Any dialogue with two speakers

In this activity

In small groups students invent a new character and write him/her into the dialogue; the audience works out who the new character is.

Preparation

Prepare a Personal Information Sheet like the one given, and make one copy for every three students.

In class

1. When people are having a conversation they always have some information about each other; even complete strangers can guess things about the other by looking at their clothes, hearing their accent, etc. Point out that this social knowledge affects how people talk to each other. You might want to bring in photographs of different kinds of people and ask students how they might address them and talk to them.

2. In groups of three, students create a new third character for the dialogue. Each group member takes a blank sheet of paper and writes at the top a name for the character. They then fold down the top of the sheet (to hide the name) and pass it on to the next member who writes the age, folds down the sheet, etc. (as in the English game, 'Consequences'), until they have got all the information covered in the Personal Information Sheet.

3. Students unfold the three sheets they have just filled in, choose the best combination of items from these three, and put them together on one Personal Information Sheet, which you hand out. This is now the new character.

Personal Information Sheet

1. NAME: ....

2. AGE: ....

3. HIGHEST EDUCATION: ....

4. JOB/PROFESSION: ....

5. RELATIONSHIP TO THE OTHER TWO CHARACTERS
   (e.g., relative, friend, colleague, boss, stranger)
   (a) to the first speaker: ....
   (b) to the second speaker: ....

6. ONE DISTINCTIVE PERSONALITY FEATURE: ....
   (e.g., ice hockey maniac; hates animals; talks too much; very greedy
   or bossy, etc.)

---

4. Students write the new character into the dialogue. Apart from the name, they should *not* mention directly any information from the sheet, e.g., should not make the new character say, *'Granny! That meal looks wonderful to a twenty-year-old engineer like me!'*, but rather they should try to make these details come through in the way the character talks and is talked to.

5. As each group performs their new version of the dialogue, the other groups work out who the new character is and jot down their guesses for the details in the Personal information sheet.

6. After each performance, compare the audience's ideas about the new character with the performers' Personal Information Sheet. How well did the performers portray the new character?

Follow-up options

1. You can turn the activity into a game if you award points to the group which has just performed for each correct detail about the new character given by each student in the audience. The winner is the group whose performance elicited the most correct answers.

2. If most of the audience cannot guess a certain detail about the new character, discuss how that detail could have been better reflected in the performance.

3. An alternative for Stage 2 can be that students first find a picture in a magazine for the new character and then fill in the Personal Information Sheet based on the photo.

Character Sheet

	Speaker 1	Speaker 2	Speaker 3	etc.
Name				
Age				
Education				
Job				
Family				
Appearance				
Taste in clothes				
Taste in music				
Favourite food				
Hobbies/interest				
Distinctive feature				

Variation 1   Get to know your characters better

Students add depth and realism to the dialogue by creating detailed personal information about the speakers. Each pair or group has a Character Sheet like the one given. First, they fill in the information they know from the dialogue. Then they go round and take turns to add a detail each until all the slots have been filled in. They could also cut out faces for each character from magazines, etc. The pairs or groups then rewrite the dialogue, adding some personal touches based on their Character Sheet. When they perform, the others say what they think has changed about the language and content of the dialogue and try to say something about the personalities of the characters.

Variation 2   Cocktail party

Each student invents an interesting, peculiar, colourful etc. character and fills in a Character Sheet for him or her. The sheets are then collected together and everybody picks one at random. All the students are invited to a cocktail party where they have to be the character on their sheet. Encourage them to circulate and talk to as many different people as they can.

Link

Consider trying **Let's not be so polite! (32)** and **Formal–informal (33)** from this section as a follow-up to this activity.

Teacher's diary

Which personal detail did students find most difficult to include in the dialogue? Were there any differences between how students indicated certain details (based on their own experience), and how these features are typically reflected in Anglo-Saxon culture?

---

31   Another time, another place . . .

Level	Intermediate and advanced
Purpose	Explore how conversation is affected by time and environment
Dialogue type	Dialogue in which the time and place of the conversation is obvious

In this activity

Students imagine that the dialogue is taking place at a different time and place, and make the necessary changes to the conversation; the audience guesses the new time and place.

Preparation

1. Establish for yourself where and when the original dialogue takes place, e.g., on the beach in Wales in July.

2. Write down some alternative times and places on separate cards — that is, some cards will have a time on them, e.g., midnight or winter holidays, and some cards a place, e.g., in the pub or Alaska. There should be at least one 'time' and one 'place' card for each group.

In class

1. Present the dialogue and discuss with students when and where it takes place and how they know this from the content. Tell them they are going to change first the 'when' and then the 'where' element but keep the people and the theme as they are (as far as possible).

2. Students get into pairs or small groups depending on the number of characters in the dialogue, and each groups picks out a time card at random. Their job is to rewrite the dialogue as if it were taking place at the new time (see **Sample dialogue**).

Sample dialogue

Original time July afternoon *Original place* A beach in Wales

Paula: It's quite hot when the sun comes out, isn't it?
Monica: Mm. I think I need some more suntan oil on my shoulders.

New time Six o'clock in the morning

Paula: Look the beach is completely empty! We can sit where we
          like but we can't hire an umbrella until eight o'clock.
Monica: It'll be more than two hours before we need an umbrella. It's
          cold! I think I'll put my jumper on.

New place A bar in Paris

Paula: Oh, it's lovely and warm in here after the Gare du Nord!
Monica: Mm. I think I'll take my coat off. I don't usually drink
          alcohol this early in the morning.

---

3. The pairs or groups perform the first new version; the audience guesses what time was written on the cards.

4. Now the groups pick out a place card and change the dialogue further to make it happen in the new place as well as at the new time (see **Sample dialogue**).

5. Students perform the second new versions. By now the dialogue should be very different from the original. The audience guesses the new place.

Follow-up option

Get students to think of various times and places and write them in two columns on the board. Each group chooses a time and a place (any combination from the list) for another group. Alternatively, the groups can draw lots. This time they have to prepare the new version by changing both the time and the place at the same time. They might really have to use their imagination in some cases.

Variation 1   Social settings

Students explore how talking to the same person about the same thing can be totally different in a different social setting. Write on cue cards settings which vary significantly from the one in the original dialogue and which will force the characters to change their behaviour. For example:

In the original
A chat in a pub

An argument at home
A discussion at a business meeting
An ordinary everyday shop scene

A conversation between friends at
   a dinner party

On the card
At a reception at Buckingham
   Palace/the White House
In the theatre
On the beach or at a funeral
At the most elegant boutique
   in town or in a run-down
   second hand shop
At the office where they both
   work

Students act out their situation and the audience must guess where it takes place.

Link

Consider trying **Change without changing (26)** from the Functions and meanings in conversation section and **Formal–informal (33)** from this section as a follow-up to this activity.

Teacher's diary

Which factor, time or place, did students find more difficult to change and why? How far were students able to keep the theme of the conversation unchanged when the time and place changed? Did they make any appropriate paralinguistic changes like changing a character's tone of voice or gestures?

---

32 Let's not be so polite!

Level   Intermediate and advanced

Purpose   Focus on the features that make speech polite and the
                   effect of politeness on conversation

Dialogue type Dialogue containing polite exchanges, preferably typical
                   politeness formulae

In this activity

Students prepare a new version of the dialogue by reducing the level of politeness.

Preparation

1. Select a short exchange from a dialogue that the students know which contains
   polite and tactful talk (as many textbook dialogues do).

2. Look at INPUT 28 and select the strategies which you would like to teach your
   students; make a copy of the Input for each student.

3. Prepare one or two less polite versions of the exchange by changing the script
   so that the speakers abandon politeness and say what they want to say in a way
   that is too direct or simply rude (see **Sample dialogue**). Input 28 gives some
   ideas of what to change and how.

Sample dialogue

Original

A: I'm sorry to bother you, Frank, but do you think you could find
   time to type this for me please? I'd be very grateful.
B: Of course, David. No problem at all.

New version

A: Type this, will you, Frank.
B: Well, all right, if I have to; but more work is about the last thing I
   need now.

INPUT 28   Common politeness strategies with examples

1. If you impose, i.e., bother the hearer or invade his/her privacy

   apologise · *I'm terribly sorry to disturb you at a time like this, but ...*

   indicate reluctance · *I hate to bother you, but ...*

   give a very strong reason · *There's simply no-one else I could ask ...*

   make the imposition seem less than it is · *Could I make a very quick phone call please? I won't be a second.*

2. If you make requests, give options for the other person to refuse without sounding rude · *It would be really nice if you could, but don't worry if you don't have time ...*

3. Ask for something in an unhopeful way so that refusal simply confirms your pessimism · *I don't suppose you'd have time to check these over ... ?*

4. Be indirect, especially when giving negative responses · *Well you're right in a way, but it's not quite as simple as that.*

5. In negative answers emphasise any positive element you can find · *Well, you've got the general idea, and this bit is really good, but I'm afraid ...*

6. Notice and attend to the hearer's interests, wants and needs · *Thanks for bringing that for me. By the way, is that a new dress?*

7. Exaggerate interest, approval or sympathy with the hearer · *Oh no! It must have been awful! Poor you standing there ... !*

8. Make the hearer feel good by

   saying what he/she would like to hear (even if you don't agree) · *Jeanie! I can't believe it! You haven't changed at all in the last thirty years!*

   giving compliments and praise · *The reason I asked you is because you're so good at organising things ...*

9. And finally, smile and nod as much as you reasonably can!

In class

1. Students listen while you read out the sample exchange and then the less polite version(s). What differences can they point out? Someone will certainly notice that the first exchange was more polite and longer than the second.

2. Discuss what language made the original exchange polite, what changes you made and the effect of those changes. What other ways do students know to make conversation polite?

3. Hand out copies of INPUT 28 and go through it briefly. How many of the politeness strategies did students mention? Ask students to read through the main dialogue and underline the parts where politeness strategies are used; check these together.

4. Students get into pairs or groups. Their task is to rewrite the dialogue by abandoning the politeness strategies and making the characters say what they might really say if they were not polite.

5. Students perform their impolite versions of the dialogue.

Follow-up options

1. Ask the students to go through some dialogues they already know and write out all the politeness forms they can find. You may also play authentic or semi-authentic taped dialogues for the same purpose.

2. For homework, each student writes out a polite exchange from a dialogue and prepares two versions of it, (a) impolite/brusque, (b) too polite.

Variation 1   Be more polite

This time students increase the level of politeness in the dialogue, which is perhaps more difficult than reducing it. Before the activity, discuss with them the main strategies which can be used to convey politeness (see INPUT 28). An example of what they are to do would be changing the sentence, *'Julie, could I borrow your tape recorder, please?'* into *'Excuse me, I'm sorry to disturb you, Julie, I know how busy you are, but could I possibly trouble you for a tape recorder? I will only need it for an hour, at the most ... '* This could be a competition: which group or pair can produce the most polite version?

Link

Consider trying **I'm afraid I can't (9)** from the Conversational rules and structure section, **What they say and what they mean (27)** from the Functions and meanings in conversation section, and Variation 2 in **How wouldn't it go at home (35)** from this section as a follow-up to this activity.

Teacher's diary

Which politeness strategy did students most often choose and change? Were there any forms or functions they were reluctant to use, for example because they considered them embarrassing, odd, or culturally different? Which of their versions sounded more natural: the very polite or the impolite?

---

33 Formal–informal

Level   Advanced

Purpose   Focus on the difference between formal and informal styles

Dialogue type Any dialogue

In this activity

Students strip down the dialogue to the basics, then dress it up in a highly formal and/or a very informal way.

Preparation

1. Look at INPUT 29, Typical differences between formal and informal speech. Select the items you would like to teach to your students. You may want to add some items of your own.

2. Take a short dialogue and prepare three new versions of it: (a) reduce each sentence to a maximum of three keywords, (b) extend these contracted lines making the style highly informal and (c) very formal (see **Sample dialogue**).

In class

1. Ask students to compare and contrast the following two sentences: *'Tom is a nice guy.'*, and *'Mr. Creepy is an amiable person.'* Other examples can be, *'Hi Tom, everything OK?'* and *'Good morning Mr. Creepy, how are you today?'*, or *'It's a damn nuisance!'* and *'It's extremely inconvenient.'* Who would say which to whom? At this stage you might discuss some of the differences between formal and informal speech outlined in INPUT 29.

2. Go through the dialogue with the students and decide what style it has been written in: formal, informal or neutral. Discuss how you could make the key parts, e.g., language functions like apologising, asking for information, suggesting, etc., and social formulae like greetings, addressing each other, etc., sound more formal or more informal.

INPUT 29   Typical differences between formal speech (FS) and informal speech (IFS)

IFS contains a more limited and basic vocabulary than FS; extensive use in IFS of phrasal verbs, which are often substituted in FS by less common verbs, e.g., *put off—postpone, do up—redecorate*; tendency in FS to use more Latin and Greek-based words and not their more common counterparts, e.g., *educate—teach, comprehend—understand*.

General tendency in IFS to be imprecise and use less specific vocabulary; more frequent use of 'all-purpose words', e.g., *thing, place, guy, do, be, have, fine, bad, good*; frequent use of words like *thingie, thingummajig, thingummabob, whatsisname, what-do-you-call-it, you-know-what-I-mean, doo-da*; frequent use of 'fillers' and 'hesitation devices', e.g., *well, you know*, etc. (see INPUT 11).

Tendency in IFS to exaggerate and use adjectives like *fantastic, great, super, smashing, terrible, awful, horrible*, etc.

Use of slang, swear words and colloquial expressions in IFS; fewer words and topics are taboo in IFS than in FS.

Most language functions have different set formulae in IFS and FS, e.g., IFS: *'Can you open the window, please?'* FS: *'Would you be so kind as to open the window, please?'*.

Politeness formulae are less emphasised and shorter in IFS than in FS, e.g., *'Thanks'* instead of *'Thank you very much'*; FS in general tends to be more polite than IFS (see INPUT 28).

In IFS people are typically addressed by their first names or nicknames, in FS by their surname preceded by some title, e.g., *Professor, Dr, President, Mrs*, etc.

IFS contains simpler grammar than FS: complicated grammatical structures and long, complex sentences are avoided.

IFS contains many ungrammatical forms, which are often the result of reducing sentences, e.g., by omitting the subject, *'Must be off'*, *'Sounds great'*, the auxiliary verb, *'Seen Joe?'*, *'You know what?'* or the verb 'to be', *'Lovely day'*, *'Good idea'*.

IFS is generally shorter, more concise and direct than FS.

IFS typically contains more personal information than FS, e.g., IFS: *'I'm going to the doctor's about my ear problem'*, FS: *'I have a doctor's appointment'*.

3. The class prepares together a skeleton version of the dialogue (see **Sample dialogue**, Version 1), which you write on the board.

4. In pairs or groups students prepare first a very informal and then a very formal version of the dialogue by extending the skeleton version on the board. (Present your sample dialogues as an illustration.) Alternatively, some groups can prepare the formal, others the informal version (perhaps they can choose).

5. The new versions are read or acted out.

Sample dialogue

Original

Paul: Hello, Victor! We're just going out for a drink. Would you like to come?

Victor: Thank you, I'd love to but Nora and I have invited some people for dinner tonight.

Version 1 (keyword skeleton)

Paul: Hello ... drink ... come ... ?

Victor: ... love ... but ... dinner ...

Version 2 (highly informal)

Paul: Hi, Vic! Coming down the pub?

Victor: Thanks, sounds great, but friends are coming round for dinner tonight.

Version 3 (very formal)

Paul: Good evening, Mr. Roe. Would you care to join us for a drink at the 'Red Lion'?

Victor: Thank you, that's most kind of you, but my wife and I are expecting dinner guests shortly.

Follow-up options

1. When students prepare their formal and informal dialogues, ask them to write three of the sentences in the wrong style, e.g., three informal sentences in the formal version. The other students must identify these stylistic odd ones out. To make the job harder for the others, students might only change one or two words within a sentence to the wrong style.

2. This book contains many lists of phrases to be used for different conversational purposes. Put several phrases from a list on the board/OHP and ask students to divide them into three categories: those which can be used between

    (a) two friends (informal),
    (b) private person, customer, client, etc. and official, clerk, shop assistant, etc. (neutral or slightly formal),
    (c) worker, employee, etc. and director, boss, etc. (highly formal).

    Note that some phrases could fall into more than one category. Lists which lend themselves to this task are INPUTS 12, 14, 22, 24 and 27 (see index **E. List of input boxes of conversational phrases**).

Variation 1   The weird interpreter

Students get into groups according to the number of speakers in the dialogue plus one extra, the weird interpreter. This person's job is to 'interpret' what each speaker says, but rather than just reformulating the sentences, he or she must change the whole style, making some sentences more formal and some more informal.

Link

Consider trying **Buying time: fillers (11)** from the Conversational strategies section, Variation 1 in **Change without changing (26)** from the Functions and meanings in conversation section, and **Let's not be so polite! (32)** from this section as a follow-up to this activity.

Teacher's diary

Did the students feel more comfortable with the formal language than the informal? Did any of them use swear words or ungrammatical forms in their informal versions, or did they feel that only native speakers can get away with speaking like that?

---

34   Family version

Level	Intermediate and advanced
Purpose	Prepare a personalised version of the dialogue and explore the language changes
Dialogue type	Dialogue that does not contain too much factual conversation, i.e., not a business transaction such as buying a train ticket, and which has preferably more than two characters

In this activity

Students rewrite the dialogue as though it was happening in their own home, between members of the family or flatmates.

Preparation

1. Go through the dialogue (or possibly several dialogues) you are going to give your students, and mark the parts (a) which sound too formal or polite to take place between family members, and (b) where more information is given than people would give to those they know well.

2. Take a short exchange from another textbook dialogue and prepare a personalised family version of it (see **Sample dialogue**) to illustrate to students what they are going to be doing.

In class

1. Ask students to read through the dialogue(s) and do what you did in the preparation: mark the parts which indicate that the conversation is not taking place at home among family members.

2. Students get into small groups depending on the number of characters in the dialogue. First of all, working individually within the group, they each rewrite the dialogue as though it took place in their own home, between members of their own family.

Sample dialogue

Original

Penny: Aren't you cold? I'm freezing. Do you mind if I close
                 the window?
Zoë: 'Course not, go ahead.
Michael: Oh sorry, I opened it. I thought it had got a bit stuffy
                 in here.
Penny: Well, we can leave it open if you like — I'll go and
                 put on my cardigan.
Michael: No, no. That's all right. Do close it.
Zoë: It was getting a bit cold, anyway.

New, personalised version

Alison Warden: Who opened the window?! I'm freezing. (She closes
                 it.)
Tom Warden: Hey! Leave that open! It's like an oven in here and
                 you can smell Dad's tennis shoes!
Mr. Warden: Watch it, cheeky, or you won't be borrowing my car
                 this evening.
Tom Warden: Just a joke, Dad! Open that window, Alison!
Alison Warden: Do it yourself!
Mr. Warden: Alison, do you have to be deliberately annoying? Open
                 it and put a sweater on if you're cold.

---

3. The groups come together and compare the three or four versions of the dialogue
    they have. Then they choose one to perform for the other groups. The student
    who has written that one becomes the 'director', filling in the background details
    for the others and helping them to play the parts of member of his/her family
    (of course, he/she will play him/herself).

4. Students perform the family versions of the dialogues and discuss them as a class.

Follow-up options

1. At home, students write up their own family versions neatly on a separate piece
    of paper and hand them in to you. In the next class, get the students into different
    groups than last time and, with their permission, give each group a family version
    to perform (without telling them whose family it is). The class then guesses whose
    family it is.

2. This time, students imagine how the dialogue would be if it took place in the home of someone they all know of, e.g., you (the teacher), a famous person, the Queen or President, etc. Then, in groups, they rewrite the dialogue accordingly, and perform the new versions.

Variation 1   What if it was you?

In groups according to the number of characters in the dialogue, each student takes a role and rewrites it as though the character was himself/herself, expressing his/her own personality. Then the group comes together and polishes the parts so that the dialogue flows logically. Remind students to change the names as well. The new versions are then performed.

Link

Consider trying **Let's not be so polite! (32), Formal–informal (33)** and **How would it go at home? (35)** from this section as a follow-up to this activity.

Teacher's diary

What were the most common changes students made to personalise the dialogue? Did the new versions sound natural? Did they find the activity interesting and challenging?

---

35 How would it go at home?

Level   Intermediate and advanced

Purpose   Explore the social and cultural elements of conversation

Dialogue type Dialogue containing some cultural information

In this activity

Students rewrite the dialogue as if the conversation were taking place in their own country, making the appropriate cultural changes.

Preparation

1. Select a dialogue, or perhaps more than one, which students already know and which contains some cultural information about the English-speaking country, people, society, etc., it deals with (since many textbook dialogues do, this should not be too difficult).

2. Mark the parts of the dialogue which you feel are particularly culture-specific, e.g., proper names, mention of prices, shop names, car names, greetings and politeness formulae, etc. Ask yourself, for example, 'How do I know this dialogue takes place in Britain and not Sweden or East Africa?'.

In class

1. Ask students to read through the dialogue(s) and make a note of all the things in it which tell you where it takes place and what nationality the speakers are. Write these things on the board as a reminder. If students do not immediately find very many, you could help them by asking, *'Do you think these people could be Mexican or Japanese or Russian, etc.?'. 'Why (not)?'*

2. Now ask students to consider what would be different about the dialogue if it took place in their own country and their own language. They should think especially about the reminders on the board.

3. If your class is multilingual, ask students to get into groups of the same nationality, or cultural or linguistic background, e.g., all Spanish speakers together, etc. If

the class is monolingual, get students into pairs or groups depending on how many speakers there are in the dialogue.

4.   Students rewrite the dialogue as though it was taking place in their own country or language. Remind them that besides the factual differences they may want to change certain things about the speakers' style and behaviour (see **Sample dialogue**).

Sample dialogue

Original

Susan: Hello John! I haven't seen you for ages!
John: Oh hi, Susan! How are you?
Susan: Fine thanks. And you?
John: Fine, fine. How's the new job at Smithson Plastics?
Susan: Oh, it's great. It's quite tiring, but the people I'm working with are really nice.

A Hungarian version

Zsuzsa: Hi!
János: Hi! It's a long time since I've seen you. How's your new job at Hungoplast?
Zsuzsa: Oh, you know, it's not bad. My salary is higher now.
János: Yes? How much do you get?
Zsuzsa: 25 000 forints, gross.

---

5.   Groups perform the new version of the dialogue. Those watching should note down for each performance what they think the three most striking differences are between the original dialogue and the culturally adapted versions.

6.   Compare and discuss what students have noted about the performances.

Follow-up option

It is worth making this exercise into a real performance where students bring in props (typical objects from their own country, if possible), dress as they really would if they were the characters in such a dialogue, and pay attention to the gestures and facial expressions they would make during conversation in their own language.

Variation 1   Too good to be true

Instructional dialogues usually paint a picture of the target language society and culture which is simply too good to be true! For example, if the dialogue takes place in the shop, the shop assistant is always polite and the shop has never run out of what the customer wants! Ask students to imagine that the dialogue is taking place in their own country and to add some less glamorous and more realistic cultural details.

Variation 2   Politeness in your country

Politeness is one of the most culture-sensitive elements in conversation. Get the students to go through the English politeness strategies described in INPUT 28, and decide which strategies are valid in their own culture; they should also think of politeness strategies in their own language which do not exist in English. Ask them to rewrite the dialogue as if it took place in their own country and, at the same time, increase the level of politeness in it.

Link

Consider trying **Cultural differences and taboos (36)** and **Visitor from Mars (37)** from this section as a follow-up to this activity.

Teacher's diary

What cultural differences did students emphasise in their performances? Had you noticed any of these differences when the students spoke in English before doing this activity with them? Were some students embarrassed to point out negative elements about their own culture?

---

36   Cultural differences and taboos

Level	Intermediate and advanced
Purpose	Raise awareness of crosscultural differences and how these affect conversation
Dialogue type	Any non-factual dialogue, i.e., not a typical shop scene, a waiter—customer exchange, etc.

In this activity

Students discuss English conversational and cultural conventions, then perform the dialogue by deliberately making some cultural mistakes; the audience must spot these.

Preparation

1. Go through the list of cultural conventions and taboos in INPUT 30 and (a) select the ones you agree with and would like to draw your students' attention to, and (b) add further items that are not included. If you teach a non-British dialect of English, then the list may need to be completely revised.

2. Either make copies of the final list for your students or put it on an OHP transparency.

INPUT 30   Some British (middle class) conversational and cultural dos and don'ts

Do not ask: how much someone earns; how much something they bought cost; about a stranger's political stance (or reveal your own directly); personal questions, such as how old someone is or whether they are married; do not mention toilet and sex too openly; do not respond to *'How are you?'* by starting to talk about your headache or digestion problems.

In conversations there is very little simultaneous talk or overlap between two speakers; some interruption is allowed, especially to ask for repetition or explanation, but too much is considered impolite.

Silences are to be avoided; a question should be followed by an answer without any delay; talking very little, not initiating topics, or giving very

---

INPUT 30 (*continued*)

brief answers may imply unfriendliness or a lack of interest.

Apart from between close friends or family, avoid direct criticism, blunt disagreement and any other conflict, e.g., no political arguments; in general avoid bluntness and heated emotions.

Politely performed negative answers, polite disagreement and conveyance of bad news are accepted (unlike in some oriental cultures).

Going off the point is not encouraged; try to be concise, direct and to-the-point; objectivity and truth are expected in most circumstances; avoid boasting; the natural reaction is to be modest.

Compliment people, e.g., on a new dress, hairstyle, etc., and respond to others' compliments by thanking them or being modest.

Do not say *'Good appetite'* before starting to eat (the French *'Bon appetit'* is used but not commonly); after a meal say thank you and compliment the host or hostess on the food.

Say *'Excuse me'* after sneezing (other people might say *'Bless you'*); blowing one's nose in public is accepted, but belching and spitting are not.

Indicate that you are listening with frequent but not constant reactions, e.g., nodding, encouraging noises and phrases; make sure there is regular eye contact with your communication partner.

Smile a lot; it is considered polite behaviour.

Avoid physical contact, except for shaking hands; there is hardly any kissing as a greeting except between family and friends; do not get too close and leave enough personal space; say *'Excuse me'* if you brush past somebody even if you do not actually touch the person.

No loud shouting, snapping fingers or clapping hands to call the waiter in a restaurant.

Be on time and not early or late.

In class

1. Very often students know quite a lot about the culture behind the language they are learning, even without ever having been to a country where that language is spoken. Ask them to brainstorm things you should not do or say in English conversation and list their ideas.

2. Introduce the list of conversational and cultural dos and don'ts you have prepared; see which ones students have mentioned and discuss the new ones.

3. Students get into pairs or groups and prepare a new version of the dialogue by including a minimum of three elements which break standard cultural rules in English conversation.

4. The pairs or groups perform their versions; the others watch the performances and jot down the cultural 'mistakes' or oddities they notice. Discuss these after each performance.

Follow-up options

1. Get students into small groups according to nationality if you have a multicultural group; ask them to go through the list of English dos and don'ts again and mark the ones which are different in their own culture(s). Then ask them to collect further differences between the English and their own culture. The list of typical culture-senstive issues in INPUT 31 may give some ideas.

INPUT 31   General culture-sensitive issues worldwide

food, eating, table manners, dinner parties, inviting guests; tipping, e.g., in restaurants, hairdressers', etc.;

superstitions, e.g., black cats crossing the road in front of you (which in Britain is considered lucky by some);

greetings, social formulae, forms of addressing people;

how different language functions are performed, e.g., apologies, compliments, requests, suggestions, agreement, disagreement; how to say 'No';

what polite behaviour involves;

how men and women treat each other, e.g., do men let women through doorways first? who do you shake hands with first, the woman or the man? what is the role of the woman/man in the family? who handles the money?

how children are treated; what's allowed and forbidden;

how old people are treated and considered;

the role of the traditional social hierarchy; what you must and must not say/do in the company of a person of a higher status;

how much people reveal of themselves in public;

how positive and negative emotions are expressed;

facial expressions, eye movements gestures, e.g., when you do not understand, when you want to interrupt, when you listen;

body movement, gestures, e.g., position of limbs when sitting, etc.

---

2. Students prepare an 'official class list' which contains all the cultural differences between the variety of English they are learning and their own culture. Give it a title, e.g., 'Cultural differences between American English and Hungarian'. A multicultural class will need more than one list. The class list(s) could be displayed on the wall and you may also want to encourage students to keep thinking of further examples and adding them to the list(s) later.

Variation 1   Crosscultural echo

Get students into small groups so that there is one group member for each role in the dialogue plus one more student to be the echo. Ask them to turn one character in the dialogue into a foreigner (let us call her Rosa) who has a dual personality; Rosa 1 can speak English but inappropriately from the cultural point of view, Rosa 2 is always correct. Every sentence Rosa says should therefore be said by her culturally inappropriate self first, then by her perfect self (see **Sample dialogue**).

Sample dialogue

William: Would you like a cup of tea or coffee . . .
Rosa 1:   (interrupting) . . . yes, some coffee and cake, please.
Rosa 2:   Oh, yes please. I'd love a cup of coffee.
William: I'll bring some cake too. Or would you prefer custard tart?
Rosa 1:   Oh, er . . . I don't know. It doesn't matter.
Rosa 2:   No, thank you. The cake sounds lovely, thanks.
William: OK. I'll be right back.
Rosa 1:   Oh, William! Where's the toilet?
Rosa 2:   Oh, sorry, but could I wash my hands first?
William: Sure, the bathroom's the first on the right.

Variation 2   Cultural understanding

Ask students to choose one or two things each they find most difficult to understand or accept about the culture behind the variety of English they are learning. Write their suggestions on the board and have the class take a vote on which one(s) they find oddest. Then students get into groups of three. Assign each group one item from among the ones they found most odd; ask them to take a positive, understanding position towards this cultural phenomenon and to prepare arguments in favour of it for the class.

Link

Consider trying **Let's not be so polite! (32), How would it go at home? (35)** and **Visitor from Mars (37)** from this section, as a follow-up to this activity.

Teacher's diary

Did the students' own culture turn out to be very different from the culture of the English dialect they are learning? If so, do you think it would help them to focus on the similarities rather than the differences? Do crosscultural differences significantly hinder your students' progress? Can you think of exercises to overcome the major difficulties?

37   Visitor from Mars

Level	Intermediate and advanced
Purpose	Explore the social and cultural aspects of conversation; practise several of the strategies and microskills introduced in earlier chapters
Dialogue type	Any dialogue, preferably with two speakers

In this activity

Students introduce a Martian visitor into the dialogue, who has none of the social or cultural background of the other speakers and keeps asking questions and making mistakes.

Preparation

1. Draw up a list which contains a few facts about the English knowledge of the Martian visitor (let us call him/her/it *Ug*), plus any other information you consider important (see Guide). Make enough copies for one between three students.

Guide to Ug's English language background

Ug's English is not very advanced; it learnt English by itself from (Martian records of) an outdated grammar book and English–Martian vocabulary lists which included only words with an equivalent in Martian.

Ug's speech is always very 'correct', e.g., it uses no contracted forms.

Ug's speaks with a monotonous intonation, i.e., all on one level.

Ug takes the literal meaning of everything and does not understand hidden meanings.

Since population is strictly controlled and social gatherings are discouraged on Mars, Ug has no understanding of social conventions in conversation.

Martians are hermaphrodites so there is no male and female, just 'it', which naturally affects communication.

Ug is very eager to learn and asks questions all the time.

---

2. Prepare one or two short dialogues (see **Sample dialogues**) in which the other characters explain to Ug what it does not understand or cannot relate to.

In class

1. Introduce Ug to the students and hand out copies of your list. You might ask students to draw Ug, too.) Discuss what kind of problems Ug might have in a conversation with English-speaking humans, remembering that Ug does speak and understand some English but has no idea about social and cultural things like being polite, or what to do in a shop, etc.

2. Show students your short dialogues and tell them that their job will be to transform the dialogue in the same way.

3. In groups of three, two human characters and Ug, students decide which parts of the dialogue would pose problems for Ug and write in the questions Ug might ask and the explanations Ug receives. The human characters should be sympathetic and not lose patience!

4. The groups perform their versions. Remind the Ugs to forget all they know about English intonation!

Sample dialogue 1

Original

Jenny: This is a nice place. Not too crowded.
Bob: Let's ask if we can sit there by the window.
Waiter: Good evening sir, madam . . .

New version

Jenny: This is a nice place. Not too crowded.
Ug: 'Crowded' — what is that?
Jenny: It's when there are lots of people. But you see, this restaurant is not crowded.
Ug: This is untrue. There are lots of people.
Bob: Don't worry, Ug. Let's ask if we can sit there by the window.
Waiter: Good evening, sir, madam . . .
Ug: Good evening, sir, madam.
Bob: Ug! He's the waiter. You mustn't call him sir or madam.
Ug: Waiter called you sir, madam, and your name is not sir, madam; it is Bob . . .

Sample dialogue 2

Original

Geoff:	Could I have a Times, please, and some chewing gum.
Shopkeeper:	Er, I'm afraid we haven't got any chewing gum . . .

New version

Geoff:	Could I have a Times, please, and some chewing gum.
Ug:	What are these things you asked him for?
Geoff:	The times is a newspaper, you know, where you can read about what's happening in the world, and chewing gum . . . ? Well, it tastes nice and . . . and you chew it but don't swallow it.
Ug:	I will never understand human things.
Shopkeeper:	Er, I'm afraid we haven't got any chewing gum.
Ug:	Why is he afraid? Are there enemies nearby? . . .

Follow-up options

1. Compare and discuss the things students picked out as being difficult for Ug to understand.

2. Imagine the same dialogue taking place a few years later after Ug has had some time to learn about Earth society and culture. Which things has Ug easily adapted to and which does Ug still have difficulty with? Students rewrite the dialogue to show this.

Variation 1   Martian conversation in English

(It might be useful for students to go through INPUTS 30 and 31 before doing this exercise.) Using the **Guide** and their imaginations, students make up a set of rules for *Martian* conversation and rewrite the dialogue (in English but as Martians would say it) as though it was taking place between Ug and one or two of its fellow Martians on Earth. This will involve changing the original dialogue a lot. Encourage the students to use Martian gestures and facial expressions, too!

Link

Consider trying **Turn-taking in conversation (7)** from the Conversational rules and structure section, and **Who is the new one? (30)** and **Cultural differences and taboos (36)** from this section as a follow-up to this activity.

Teacher's diary

How did students react to Ug? Did you find that those students who are more open to foreign cultures and people handled this activity better and took it more seriously? Did this activity help students become more conscious of conversational conventions?

INDEXES

A. The teaching purpose of the activities

147

Section II: Conversational strategies

No.	Title	Teaching Point	Page

Section IV: Social and cultural contexts

No.	Title	Teaching Point	Page
30	WHO IS THE NEW ONE?	Status, office and personal style in conversation	114
V.1	Get to know your characters better	Adding personal details about the characters in the dialogue	116
V.2	Cocktail party	Working out personal styles for given characters in a given social setting	116
31	ANOTHER TIME, ANOTHER PLACE ...	The effect of time and environment on conversation	118
V.1	Social settings	Conversation and different social settings	119
32	LET'S NOT BE SO POLITE!	Politeness strategies	121
V.1	Be more polite	Politeness strategies	123
33	FORMAL—INFORMAL	Formal and informal styles	125
V.1	The weird interpreter	Formal and informal styles	128
34	FAMILY VERSION	Personalising the dialogue	129
V.1	What if it was you?	Personalising the dialogue	131
35	HOW WOULD IT GO AT HOME?	Social and cultural elements of conversation	132
V.1	Too good to be true	Introducing less glamorous and more realistic cultural elements into the dialogue	133
V.2	Politeness in your country	Crosscultural differences in politeness strategies	134
36	CULTURAL DIFFERENCES AND TABOOS	The effect of crosscultural differences on conversation	135
V.1	Crosscultural echo	Crosscultural blunders	138
V.2	Cultural understanding	Understanding odd cultural phenomena	138
37	VISITOR FROM MARS	Social and cultural aspects of conversation; using strategies and microskills introduced earlier	140
V.1	Martian conversation in English	Contrasting English conversational conventions with imaginary Martian rules	142

B. Short summaries of activities

Activity	Summary	Page
Adding a point (3, V.1)	Students practise interrupting their conversation partner to add a point	15
ANOTHER TIME, ANOTHER PLACE ... (31)	The dialogue is changed to a new time and place; the audience guesses where and when.	118
ARE YOU LISTENING? (15)	Speaker B is not listening and an irritated Speaker A must keep asking 'attention-regaining questions.	58
Are you still there? (15, V.1)	In a telephone conversation, one speaker is slow to react so the other must ask questions to check whether he/she is listening	59
Be more polite (32, V.1)	Students rewrite the dialogue by increasing the level of politeness.	123
Be over-sensitive (28, V.1)	One speaker finds hidden offensive meanings in the other's words and must be constantly reassured.	105
BUYING TIME: FILLERS (11)	The speakers delay their answers by using fillers and hesitation devices.	44
BY THE WAY, THAT REMINDS ME (2)	Students extend the dialogue by introducing new topics.	10
Can't say goodbye (10, V.2)	A man and a woman cannot say goodbye to each other.	39
Change-the-subject chain (2, V.2)	Students receive cue cards with topics, and they change the subject from the previous speaker's topic to their own.	12
CHANGE WITHOUT CHANGING (26)	Students alter every sentence of the dialogue, but leave the meaning intact.	98
Cocktail party (30, V.2)	Students pretend to be funny characters at an imaginary cocktail party.	116
Crosscultural echo (36, V.1)	One character has a culturally proper and improper self, and all his/her parts are said by both selves.	138

Activity	Summary	Page
Cultural understanding (36, V.2)	Students vote for the oddest cultural aspect of the target language, then in groups prepare a case supporting that cultural aspect.	138
CULTURAL DIFFERENCES AND TABOOS (36)	Students perform the dialogue, deliberately making some cultural mistakes; the audience must spot these.	135
DIALOGUE HALVES (5)	Half of the students are given a dialogue without Speaker A's part, the other half without Speaker B's part; they provide the missing parts then match these new dialogue halves.	19
Difficult to disagree (24, V.1)	A character is added to a conversation who agrees all the time with one speaker, making the job of the other who disagrees even harder.	92
Do I make myself understood?! (14, V.1)	One speaker is angry with the other and tells him/her off, giving warnings.	56
Don't get me wrong! (16, V.1)	One speaker in the dialogue misunderstands something and is about to take offence, so the other tries to sort out the problem.	63
Embarrassing silence (8, V.2)	One character is unresponsive, which forces the other to do all the talking to avoid silences.	30
Enquiring over the phone (22, V.1)	Students add questions to ask for information on the telephone.	86
FAMILY VERSION (34)	Students rewrite the dialogue as though it was happening in their own home and their family or friends were the participants.	129
FORMAL–INFORMAL (33)	Students prepare a very formal and a very informal version of the dialogue.	125
Get to know your characters better (30, V.1)	Students fill in a Character sheet by inventing details about the characters in the dialogue, then they change the text to match the personalities they have created.	116
GOING OFF THE POINT (19)	One speaker deliberately goes off the point and evades questions.	71
How embarrassing! (11, V.1)	Students get cue cards with an embarrassing situation and they introduce this element into the dialogue, using fillers.	46
How to be irritating (29, V.1)	Students break conversation rules to be deliberately irritating, causing conflict.	109
HOW TO DISAGREE POLITELY (24)	One of the characters disagrees politely with what the other is saying.	90
HOW WOULD IT GO AT HOME? (35)	Students rewrite the dialogue as if the conversation were taking place in their own country, making the appropriate cultural changes.	132

Activity	Summary	Page
Human dialogue chain (6, V.1)	Students are each given one section of a dialogue, and by listening to the others' sections, they reconstruct the text.	23
I COULDN'T GET A WORD IN EDGEWAYS! (8)	The dialogue is turned into a monologue, students make one speaker do all the talking.	28
I HAVEN'T GOT ALL DAY! (4)	A customer gets into a lively conversation with the person attending to him/her, while an impatient second customer tries to interrupt them.	16
I'M AFRAID I CAN'T (9)	One speaker chooses the more difficult response to an offer, invitation, apology, etc. (that is, turns down, shows reluctance, refuses to accept, etc.).	31
I'm sorry, the line is very bad (12, V.1)	The line is bad in a telephone conversation and the speakers keep asking for repetition.	49
IN OTHER WORDS (16)	One speaker interprets wrongly what the other has said, forcing the other to reformulate his/her message.	61
Interpreting from English into English (26, V.1)	An interpreter rephrases all the sentences in the dialogue without changing their meaning.	99
IS THAT CLEAR? (14)	One speaker is not sure whether the other is following and asks check questions.	55
IT WAS NICE TALKING TO YOU (10)	One speaker refuses to end the conversation in spite of the efforts of the other.	36
JUMBLED DIALOGUE (6)	Students rearrange the jumbled parts of a dialogue.	22
Keep the conversation going (1, V.1)	Students practise keeping up conversation by asking questions, adding opinions, telling stories, etc.	8
LET'S NOT BE SO POLITE! (32)	Students prepare a new version of the dialogue by reducing the level of politeness.	121
Let's not chat (1, V.2)	One character is eager to chat and the other tries everything to stop the conversation.	9
Martian conversation in English (37, V.1)	Students create a whole new set of conventions for Martian conversation and act out the dialogue accordingly.	142
Mime the word (18, V.1)	Students must not say certain key words in the dialogue but must use mime to elicit them from their conversation partner.	69
MORE OF THE SAME (21)	Students become 'textbook writers' and rewrite the dialogue in such a way that the functional teaching purpose becomes more featured.	82

Activity	Summary	Page
Multiple-choice dialogue (5, V.1)	Each turn in the dialogue has three versions from which students must choose the good one.	20
OH YES, I AGREE (23)	One speaker keeps expressing opinions on related topics and the other speaker politely agrees with these.	87
One-sided telephone conversation (8, V.1)	In a telephone conversation we can only hear one speaker but can guess what the other is saying too.	29
PARANOIA OR A HIDDEN MEANING IN EVERYTHING (28)	Each sentence in the dialogue is followed by an 'echo': an underlying hidden meaning of the sentence.	104
PARDON? (12)	Students perform the dialogue pretending they do not hear certain things and ask the other speaker to repeat.	47
Pet subject (19, V.1)	One speaker directs the conversation to their pet subject, regardless of the original topic.	73
Politeness in your country (35, V.2)	Students rewrite the dialogue as though it was taking place in their country and increase the level of politeness.	134
QUESTIONS AND ANSWERS (22)	One speaker asks further questions to which the other speaker does not know the answer.	84
REACTIONS (25)	Unexpected sentences are added to one speaker's part which require various reactions from the other speaker.	93
RELAX AND CHAT (1)	A short, factual exchange is turned into a conversation by broadening the topic and developing a social relationship between the speakers.	6
Reversed responses (9, V.1)	All the responses in the dialogue are reversed, e.g., if someone accepted an invitation, he/she should now turn it down.	34
Secret agents (19, V.2)	The characters become secret agents who evade questions by going off the point.	73
Social settings (31, V.1)	The social setting of the dialogue is transformed, making certain language changes necessary.	119
Sorry, I'm a language learner (13, V.2)	A language learner wants to doublecheck if he/she has understood everything correctly.	53
SORRY TO INTERRUPT (3)	Students use interrupting strategies to break into a conversation several times.	13
Stopping Uncle Freddy (2, V.1)	One character is extremely talkative and gets side-tracked all the time.	11

Activity	Summary	Page
Telephone closings (10, V.1)	One speaker makes several attempts to close a telephone conversation but the other will not stop talking!	38
The hinting game (27, V.1)	All the requests and suggestions in the dialogue become subtle, indirect hints.	102
The interrupting game (3, V.2)	One team prevents the other from reading out a text by interrupting.	15
The office game (4, V.1)	A conflict develops between a client who wants to arrange something and two bureaucrats who have a nice chat.	17
The paraphrase survey (17, V.1)	Students carry out a class-survey on which paraphrase structures are the most popular.	67
THE THING YOU OPEN BOTTLES WITH (17)	Students are not allowed to say certain key words and must overcome this difficulty with paraphrase and approximation, i.e., using an alternative word.	65
The turn-taking game (7, V.1)	Students act out the dialogue including all but one of the turn-taking strategies from their lists; the audience must spot the missing one.	27
The weird interpreter (33, V.1)	A strange interpreter interprets from English into English, mixing styles.	128
Three difficult words (13, V.1)	Three difficult words are added to a speaker's part and the other must ask for explanations	53
Titles (21, V.1)	Students first give a title to the dialogue, then rewrite it so that it suits the title even better.	83
Too good to be true (35, V.1)	Students rewrite the dialogue as though it was taking place in their country and introduce less glamorous and more realistic cultural details.	133
TURN-TAKING IN CONVERSATION (7)	Students learn about the different signals people use to indicate their turn in a conversation then fill in a turn-taking observation sheet while listening to recorded dialogues.	24
Unexpected questions (11, V.2)	Students get cue cards with embarrassing or unexpected questions which they have to include in the dialogue, forcing the other to improvise and use fillers.	46
VISITOR FROM MARS (37)	A Martian visitor (named Ug) who lacks the social and cultural background of the other speakers keeps asking questions and making mistakes.	140

C. Activities by language proficiency level

Elementary

Adding a point
ARE YOU LISTENING?
Are you still there?
BUYING TIME: FILLERS
DIALOGUE HALVES
Enquiring over the phone
How embarrassing!
Human dialogue chain
I'm sorry, the line is very bad
IS THAT CLEAR?
IT WAS NICE TALKING TO YOU
JUMBLED DIALOGUE
Mime the word
Multiple-choice dialogue
OH YES, I AGREE
PARDON?
QUESTIONS AND ANSWERS
REACTIONS
Sorry, I'm a language learner
SORRY TO INTERRUPT
Telephone closings
The interrupting game
The paraphrase survey
THE THING YOU OPEN BOTTLES WITH
Three difficult words
Unexpected questions
WHAT DO YOU CALL IT?
WHAT DO YOU MEAN?
Wrong reactions
Yes sir, I agree entirely, sir

Intermediate

ANOTHER TIME, ANOTHER PLACE . . .
BY THE WAY, THAT REMINDS ME
Can't say goodbye
Change-the-subject chain
CHANGE WITHOUT CHANGING
Cocktail party
Crosscultural echo
CULTURAL DIFFERENCES AND TABOOS
Difficult to disagree
Do I make myself understood?!
Embarrassing silence
FAMILY VERSION
Get to know your characters better
GOING OFF THE POINT
HOW TO DISAGREE POLITELY
HOW WOULD IT GO AT HOME?
I COULDN'T GET A WORD IN EDGEWAYS!
I HAVEN'T GOT ALL DAY!
I'M AFRAID I CAN'T
Interpreting from English into English
Keep the conversation going
LET'S NOT BE SO POLITE!
Let's not chat
MORE OF THE SAME
One-sided telephone conversation
PARANOIA OR A HIDDEN MEANING IN
    EVERYTHING
Pet subject
Politeness in your country
RELAX AND CHAT

Intermediate continued

Advanced

D. Subject index

E. List of input boxes of conversational phrases